Altar Ego Musings

Altar Ego Musings

By
R. K. Bohm

*MUSINGS FOR MOCCIAS
to use
and be amused —
Blessings,
Bob
R K Bohm*

E-BookTime, LLC
Montgomery, Alabama

Altar Ego Musings

Copyright © 2007 by R. K. Bohm

All rights reserved. No part of this book may be reproduced or transmitted in any form or by any means, electronic or mechanical, including photocopying, recording, or by any information storage and retrieval system, without permission in writing from the copyright owner.

ISBN: 978-1-59824-712-1

First Edition
Published October 2007
E-BookTime, LLC
6598 Pumpkin Road
Montgomery, AL 36108
www.e-booktime.com

Contents

Resurrection Rabbit	9
Which Ten Commandments?	13
Doggies in Heaven?	16
Sex a Risky Topic for Clergy	19
Talking to Strangers	22
Talking to Extraterrestrials	24
In God(s) We Trust	26
Angels and Pinheads	28
Disorganized Religion	31
The Ghostly Holiday Approaches	33
Frodo and Fantasies	34
The Limits of Prayer	36
Plain Talk with God	39
First Christmas Eve: No 'Silent Night'	41
Late for Christmas	43
A Time to Bridge Denominational Differences	45
Jesus Drives . . . A Hard Bargain	48
Church is More Than Sunday	50
A Good Book for School	53
The Dynamics of Prayer	55
'So Help Me God'	58
Candor an Unwelcome Wedding Guest	60
Lost in Space: Feel the Wonder	62
St. Patrick for Protestants	64
No 'Old Time Religion'	66
Purgatory for Protestants	69
Religion, Revolution and Evolution	71
Up from the Slime	74
Churches Should Sue	76
Earth is Our Ark	79
Noah's Ark: Truth and Fiction	81
Noah's Ark: A Two by Two Story	83
Noah's Ark: Beyond Religion	85
Noah's Ark: Don't Rock the Boat	87
Gibson Film Promises Impact Different from the Bible	89
Immortality Denied	92
New Age Responses	94
Bible Thumpers' Responses	95

Contents

Resurrection 97
Retraction, Maybe 98
Dante and Funerals 100
Dreadful Holidays 102
The Bewitching Spell of Paganism 105
When Atheists Pray 107
The Virtue of Skepticism 109
Undemocratic Scripture 111
Thanks for Creation 114
Biblical Family Values 116
Christmas Clutter 118
Marley's Ghost 120
Beware of Claus 122
Christian Chanukah 125
Smote Signals 127
Christian Friendly Fire 129
Secular Humanists 132
Good and Bad 134
Finding Relevant Commandments 136
Snow Job 139
Imagine It 141
In the Humanists' Den 144
Religious Convertibles 146
Tabloid Theology 148
Many Kinds of 'Reality' 151
A Lutheran Baptist 153
Easter Disappointment 156
Believe Which Bible? 158
Biblical Technology 161
Hand Work in the Church 163
Number of Beasts 166
The Rights Stuff 168
On the Psychic Hotline 170
Politically Correct 172
Hot as Hell? Maybe Even Hotter 175
Differing Views of God 177
Sensitive to Ethnic Jokes 179
Planetary Changes 182

Contents

God's Billboards 184
Parsing Bad Words 186
God's Will – Or Not?...189
Voices in My Head 191

Resurrection Rabbit
NVD April 16, 2003

Easter season reminds me how poorly our seminaries train us clergy for the real world. After all my intensive study of Scripture and detailed and systematic review of theology, I'm still at a complete loss about how to deal with what seems to be Easter's most important phenomenon.

I've gone to my religious dictionaries and encyclopedias of Christian thought. I've consulted obscure texts about the liturgy and esoteric volumes about Church folklore through the ages. I've asked questions at small clergy gatherings as well as at national symposia. Nowhere have I been able to learn anything about that most significant figure of Easter season: the Easter Bunny.

I even consulted a Jewish colleague with whom I had been doing some ecumenical Bible study. He made a brilliant suggestion: Since Jesus was a Jewish teacher allegedly returned from the dead on Easter, perhaps early on he was known as the "Easter Rabbi" and later, when relationships between the synagogue and church deteriorated and the church lost touch with its Jewish antecedents, the term came to be misunderstood as the "Easter Rabbit".

Nice try, but I doubted it.

St. Patrick, Ireland, and the shamrock I studied extensively. Santa Claus's descent from Nicholas, the bishop of Myra in Asia Minor, was reviewed thoroughly in my seminary classes. St. Valentine and his relationship to hearts, love, and romance we covered in detail. All Saints Day, St. Blaise and the healing of throats, St. Francis and the blessing of animals, Reformation Day and Corpus Christi, Candlemas and Michaelmas – I know all about their histories and traditions. But the Easter Bunny, for all his popularity on television, in greeting cards, in children's stories, at the shopping malls, and even in our congregations' Church School classes, seems to have been shunned and ignored by the official religious establishment.

Wherever he came from, he certainly is a persistent creature. Approaching my first church for a children's Easter egg hunt long years ago, I was surprised to see someone in a huge and colorful Easter Bunny outfit greeting the children. A young lad, all excited, ran up to me and exclaimed, "Pastor, pastor, do you know who that is?"

As I've admitted, my seminary training had its deficiencies so, in my naiveté, I took a wild guess, "It's the Resurrection Rabbit!"

The figure in costume put its paws on its hips and cocked its head at me in a very obviously disparaging gesture: "Who are you and what are you talking about?"

"No, no," the little one explained. "It's the Easter Bunny!"

And the costumed figure nodded vigorously.

"Are you sure?" I asked. "I thought it was the Resurrection Rabbit. To remind us how Jesus hopped out of the tomb on Easter Day."

More incredulous and scornful gestures from the costumed figure. Disgust from the child: "It's the Easter Bunny. To give us eggs."

Some eleven and twelve year olds already on the verge of teenage rebelliousness and obviously not happy at being dragged to an egg hunt planned for prepubescent children and starring a costumed bunny, came to my defense. They gathered menacingly around the small child and strongly advised, "The pastor says it's the Resurrection Rabbit. So it's the Resurrection Rabbit. Got it?"

The youngster got it; his friends got it; and for that year, and that year only, St. Whoever-it-was Church was visited by the Resurrection Rabbit.

But the Easter Bunny is an amazingly persistent creature. The next year my supportive eleven and twelve year olds didn't come to the Easter egg hunt. I suspected their parents were avoiding another bunny-rabbit confrontation triggered by their pastor's naivete and lack of adequate seminary training. In their absence the younger crowd gathered around me as menacingly as the older ones had gathered around them the previous year.

"Say hello to the Easter Bunny, Pastor," they strongly advised me.

Not having had relevant seminary preparation for those kinds of confrontations, I said an affable "Hello there, Easter Bunny", withered as the costumed beast condescendingly patted me on the head, and never again tried to replace him with the Resurrection Rabbit.

Seminary may not have trained me how to understand and deal with Easter Bunnies, but the young folk taught me that powerful stories, even far-fetched ones involving a rabbit who delivers colored eggs, have amazing persistence. And that survival strength certainly gives me hope for the power and persistence of the story that I tell from the pulpit every Easter.

- - - - -

Before it appeared in the *Northern Virginia Daily* in 2003, *Resurrection Rabbit* had been published in a number of other local newspapers in areas where I was serving as a Lutheran interim minister. In 1996 it was in Pennsylvania's Wilkes-Barre *Times Leader* and ten years later a member of the congregation I had been serving when I wrote it reminisced about it when I returned for a visit. As the most popular of my editorials, it has pride of place in this collection.

From here on the editorials follow their chronological sequence as they appeared in the *Northern Virginia Daily*. It would have been too difficult to arrange them by topics, since *Resurrection Rabbit* fits in both the category of "Holidays" with "Purgatory for Protestants" and "Christmas No Silent Night," and "St. Patrick for Protestants" and the category of "Christianity in confrontation with contemporary culture" with pieces like "Jesus Drives a Hard Bargain," "Religion, Revolution, and evolution," and "When Atheists Pray." So rather than shuffle them out of their chronological order and try to reassemble them according to themes, I present them for the most part in the chronological sequence of their publication.

Earlier, in the nineties, I had submitted some editorials to newspaper syndicates under the title "Altar Ego." A pun on "alter ego," it signaled, I had hoped, that my material was a playful variation on the normal religious editorial, an alternate view from the altar by someone willing to admit to having an ego.

Alas, I am so often misunderstood. Response letters from newspaper syndicates declining my submissions usually corrected my return address from "Altar Ego Publications" to "Alter Ego Publications." I guess they thought I couldn't spell and I suspect they consequently didn't even bother to read my samples. If they had, I'm sure they would have offered me a contract as a columnist.

One syndication editor, however, in a handwritten note explained that his group did not handle religious editorials but added, "Good luck getting them published elsewhere. Their name alone deserves it!" Little triumphs like that kept me writing and made possible this collection and the one that will soon follow.

My suggestion is that you leave this book in an appropriate place where you can pick it up easily on a daily basis, read two or three editorials, and then put it down until the next time you're sitting in the same place.

Lege et dilege! Read and enjoy!

Which Ten Commandments?
NVD May 22, 2002

Should the Ten Commandments be publicly posted in federal or state buildings or in classrooms to improve America's moral tone?

Clergy though I am, I doubt it.

I have problems with the Ten Commandments.

Not just problems keeping them, though certainly that, especially in the way they're interpreted by Jesus, Maimonides, Thomas Aquinas, or Martin Luther. I have other problems with them too.

Basically (don't tell my bishop!), I'm not even sure which commandments make up the ten. Exodus 20: 1-17 and Deuteronomy 5:6-21 list not TEN but eleven or twelve commandments depending how you count them. Presbyterians and Reformed or United Church of Christ folk count "Thou shalt make no graven image" as the second commandment, then lump together as one "Thou shalt not covet thy neighbor's wife" and "Thou shalt not covet thy neighbors' other stuff." Lutherans, my own denominational tradition, and Roman Catholics take the "graven images" verse not as a separate commandment, but as a subordinate part of the first commandment, and then count the two "Thou shan't covets" as two separate commandments.

Here's one problem: If we post the "Ten Commandments" on the courtroom wall or in the class room, which numbering system would be used? Would the state favor the Baptist or the Episcopalian system of counting them? Could politicians agree which denominational constituency they wanted to favor? I doubt it.

Second, as a firm believer in the importance of the Bible, I notice the Bible itself never uses the phrase "Ten Commandments". Although the phrase may be added as a page heading or chapter title in English translations, it appears nowhere in the original Hebrew or Greek texts.

Jesus, the rabbi from Nazareth, did fuss a good bit about keeping the commandments, but he never limited his discussions to only ten of them. In company with other first century rabbis he interpreted the whole 613 commandments, according to rabbinic count, not just ten. In his sermon on the mount from Matthew 5:17-48, for example, he goes from interpreting commandments about murder and adultery to interpreting commandments about divorce and swearing oaths and loving one's neighbor, which are not from among the ten. It's as if he made no distinction.

If the Bible itself and Jesus himself never use the phrase "Ten Commandments" or single them out as of primary significance, why should we?

Finally, I admit that scripture's Big Ten against murder, adultery, stealing, and false witness certainly do address some real problems in our society. But I question whether it would help to post them in public. Are those who most need them able to read them? Or read anything else for that matter?

Or, if those who most need them can read them, are they able to make the necessary connections? Will they realize that "Thou shalt not kill" might be saying something against the slow death that drug abuse can begin? Or that "Thou shalt not commit adultery" might apply not just to promiscuity but also to pornography? Would they realize that graffiti or vandalism, which destroy property, might actually be forbidden by "Thou shalt not steal"? Or that putting one's name on an examination or term paper that resulted from cheating or plagiarism violates "Thou shalt not bear false witness?"?

Again, I doubt it.

As a clergy-person I certainly think the Bible is important as the Word of God. (Tell my bishop!) But as a skeptic in the Biblical tradition of St. Thomas the Doubter, I sometimes suspect the urge to post the Ten Commandments in public buildings does not really arise from serious hopes of actually reversing society's moral decay. Does anyone really believe that posting in public places "Thou shalt not take the Divine Name in vain" will cut down on profanity? I suspect the real urge for posting the Ten Commandments is to try to fool ourselves into thinking we're doing our job, when in fact society's moral decay shows that we are not.

Further, I wouldn't single out merely ten of the six hundred thirteen commandments for special duty in courts or school. Since the Bible doesn't interpret itself (which counting system represents the real ten?) I certainly would emphasize that much more important than simply copying off some verses of the Bible is being a part of the communities that interpret the Bible. Let federal or state buildings or classrooms be posted with signs reading "Get actively involved in your synagogue or church".

- - - - -

Soon after my transition from teaching classical languages and literature at Muhlenberg College to serving as pastor at St. Timothy, Allentown, I had as one of my Sunday texts the passage in which the Sadducees, who didn't believe in the resurrection, asked Jesus to whom in the afterlife a woman would be married after having had seven husbands. Their intent was to discredit the idea of an afterlife, but Jesus responded that marital relationships didn't exist in the afterlife. For unhappily married people I was sure that news was a relief, but for happily married people I suspected it would be a disappointment. As a good company man for the Kingdom of Heaven I didn't want those happily married people complaining about the company's retirement plan, so I tried to justify the lack of marital status in the life to come.

The sermon actually had two parts, each of which was complete in itself: in addition to the reflection about marriage, I reflected a bit about pets in the afterlife, always a topic of high emotional interest but of little theological commentary. After the service five or six congregational members requested "the part of the sermon about pets." I had copies made and distributed them regularly when members were grieving over a pet. That material was written back when I was solemn and serious . . . well, more solemn and serious than I became later down the line when I wrote the following essay.

As a result of the original sermon and its circulated copies I was asked to perform "funerals" for pets, even after I left St. Timothy. My successor there, who later became a bishop, was reluctant to do that kind of ceremony. I don't understand the problem. Grieving families are grateful they had the pet and hope the pet has some kind of eternal significance or eternal "life." So into God's presence we go, remembering with thanksgiving and asking for hope and healing. However bishops may feel about it, I don't think the Creator minds.

I was glad to discover others had wrestled with the problem of pets in the afterlife. When I finally had to say goodbye to my dog Alex after seventeen years, both the veterinary in Pennsylvania where I was serving and Alex's veterinary back home in Virginia were outstandingly comforting. Dr. Bruce Coston in Virginia suggested to me in a consolation note *Will my Pet Go to Heaven?* by Steve Wohlburg. My approach is brief and Biblical; the book's approach is lengthy and theological and has my recommendation to those who want more reassurance than the following, half flippant editorial affords.

- - - - -

Doggies in Heaven?
NVD June 19, 2002

Questions from my congregations, especially from younger folk, often remind me how poorly seminary trained me for answering life's real existential issues.

"Pastor, do doggies go to heaven?" is one I get regularly, usually from a youngster in tears with a pleading look that begs me to make the church's constant talk about eternal life relevant to a first encounter with serious grief. Seminary gave me no clue, however, about doggies in heaven.

"What did your parents tell you?" I used to ask the bereaved, figuring to accomplish two worthy goals: support whatever approach the parents had taken and avoid wrestling with the need of providing my own answer.

"They said I should ask you," was the inevitable reply.

The first thirty times this happened I felt flattered by the confidence I assumed the parents were placing in my theological acumen. After that I finally came to maturity and realized they were just passing the buck.

I consulted older clergy friends.

Some said it was a ridiculous question and there was nothing in Augustine, Aquinas, Maimonides, Luther, or Calvin about it and I should ease the child's tears by saying it was an inappropriate question.

Some said I should point out to the child the obvious difference between good doggies, presumably like the departed canine, and bad doggies, then advise that if the child wanted to see the doggie ever again, the child better be very good, which included the child's demanding that his or her parents begin to tithe.

Some said that heaven was part of an antiquated mythological construct and the honest thing for me to do was to explain that to the child. Using, of course, figurative language that the child would be able to understand.

Some said that no matter how my theology – or lack thereof – handled – or ignored – the question, the paramount concern was to relieve the child's hurt and so out of pastoral care I should say "Of course they do" even if I couldn't support my answer.

Some advised me not to answer the question about doggies in heaven but to focus on the child's grief and allow its full expression.

Some help.

As so often in my ministry, I had to thrash out an answer without benefit of seminary notes. It was a serious dilemma.

Tell children of course doggies go to heaven when I was not really sure they do (though I certainly hoped so)? Might be setting the young innocent up for a major disappointment some time hereafter.

Tell children heaven doesn't include doggies and further break already broken young hearts?

Tell children I have no idea whether or not doggies go to heaven and reveal the glaring inadequacies of my seminary training?

Finally I fought my way through to an answer that I hope deals adequately with all the complexities of the question.

Whether or not the particular doggie in question made it through whatever transition is symbolically depicted by pearly gates I of course cannot answer. I don't know what doggies will be like there any more than I know what I'll be like there.

But I can testify on good Biblical grounds that the Creator of all things has a special interest in animals and in our human relationships with animals. In one of the creation stories, Genesis 2: 19-20, before humanity decides to try to be its own boss, God gives humanity the authority to name the animals, that is, to identify them, to call them, to relate with them. Our relationship with our pets has a divine sanction.

Another Biblical image, for the new scheme of things the Creator has in store for us after we leave this one that we've botched up, depicts a future in which wolves lie down with lambs, calves with lions, and a child leads them. Isaiah 11:6-9 assures us, among other things, that our relationships with animals has some kind of future when the kingdom is restored and perfected.

I was so proud of having arrived at a reasonable and Scriptural response that I even worked the answer into one section of my Christian doctrine classes for teenagers, many of whom had pets.

Once while I was presenting to a class of teenagers my fully articulated theology about doggies and heaven, one of them, hormones obviously raging as he ogled the legs of a girl in a short skirt across the aisle, asked me, "Pastor, never mind dogs; will there be sex in heaven?"

I was reminded once again how poorly seminary had prepared me for answering life's real existential questions.

- - - - -

As here, my essays often lament the inadequacy of my seminary training. I confess that's nonsense, simply my attempt, perhaps inappropriate, to win the sympathy of those who may consider seminary education too academic, esoteric, obscure, and irrelevant. I apologize to the two excellent schools from which I received my theology degrees: Princeton Theological Seminary, New Jersey, and Union Theological Seminary in New York. They may in fact not have taught me about dogs and cats in the afterlife or about sexual relations in heaven or about how to defuse a barroom brawl or about where the Easter bunny came from, but they certainly tried to teach me to think Biblically and critically and to express theological ideas clearly and compellingly. If these editorials fulfill their intended double duty of both informing and delighting, as much credit is due to those two institutions as to the author.

- - - - -

Sex a Risky Topic for Clergy
NVD July 13, 2002

Questions, especially from young folks, remind me how poorly seminary prepared me for addressing life's real existential problems.

Once in a high school Christian doctrine class a teenager, hormones obviously raging as he ogled the legs of a girl in a short skirt across the aisle, asked me, "Pastor, will there be sex in heaven?"

I could think of some parishioners who would say, "I certainly hope not!" They had been, I knew, in bad and unfortunate relationships in which sexual activities were not happy experiences, but this young fellow was certainly of quite the opposite persuasion.

I tried to deal with the question fairly and honestly. And during our ensuing discussion the class became much more attentive, didn't get restless as the end of the hour approached, hung around afterwards to continue the conversation, and pursued it further the next two times we met.

We had much material to juggle in those three sessions.

We talked about the Biblical meaning of "know" – "Then Abel knew his wife and she conceived" – and intimacy and shame and fig leaves, which led to conversation about God "knowing" us, seeing us naked, without our fig leaves, and loving us nonetheless.

We talked about the relationship between our bodies and our wills: how our bodies are sometimes rebellious against our wills, especially in regard to sexual appetites, and how "heaven" is a condition where we are no longer divided creatures with our bodies sometimes encouraging one thing and our wills objecting and resisting.

We talked about the Creator's intention that humanity have joy, pleasure, and fulfillment, which was as much of a surprise to most of them as was the concept that God had created sex in the first place.

We reviewed that "heaven" means being in full harmony with the Creator and that only when the creature is in full harmony with its Creator can she or he have the perfect joy, pleasure, and fulfillment for which we were created.

We had a lengthy digression when one girl in the class

brought up Mark 12:25, in which Jesus says that people in the new life beyond this one "Neither marry nor are given in marriage."

One fellow was quick to point out that Jesus' assertion that there was no marriage in heaven did not necessarily mean there were no sexual relationships in heaven. And that observation naturally led to a spirited discussion, amid many revealing blushes in the class, of the relationship between sexual intimacy and marriage.

By the end of the third session I was into the discussion even more than the young folk. Two of my favorite subjects were being discussed simultaneously: Bible study and sex. Thoroughly alive to the subject, I said something to the general effect that knowing and being known by our Creator after death would be a joy and pleasure of which sexual fulfillment was only a pale foreshadowing. And I might have used some terms for body parts and orgasms that were not from biology text books. The young folk didn't seem to notice or care, but obviously they mentioned it to their parents somewhere along the line.

It was very fulfilling and pleasurable the way theology, scripture, and real life all came together, so to speak, in that class. But then the proverbial fan was hit by something they don't mention by name in seminary, though they deal with a lot of it.

Word got around that the Christian doctrine class had been talking about sex. That the pastor had a real gutter mouth. That he was trying to use the pleasures of sex to interest young people in heaven.

After the Church Council got involved they invited my bishop to participate in the discussion. When all the fuss was finally over I had learned some valuable lessons besides those from discussion with the teenagers.

First, clergy should not discuss sex honestly, especially with teenagers.

Second, clergy should not use a street-wise vocabulary.

Third, if clergy do discuss sex, they should under no circumstances admit that it is pleasurable, especially to teenagers.

These valuable lessons which I learned I was soon able to take with me into my next congregation. I had been just about ready to move on anyway.

- - - - -

Skeptic that I am, I doubted that John Horan, the editor of the *Northern Virginia Daily*, would print the above sequel to "Doggies in Heaven" in its entirety, if at all. Not only did he publish the whole essay, he did it on my birthday. A good present! Thank you again, John!

Sex in the pulpit is not as rare as it used to be – I mean as a preaching topic, not a practice. Even so, if the Sunday's lessons lead me into a discussion from the pulpit of this strong human appetite, I know some people in the congregation will be unhappy. Preachers in past years seem to have given many congregants the impression that church talk, at least from the pulpit, should not engage or relate with real life concerns. Fortunately that impression is being changed.

Some things sermons traditionally did not speak about: sex, politics, and the afterlife of pets. Some things the church does speak about regularly often mean very different things to those outside the church. When the church talks, for example, about "heaven" the images in people's minds are often pearly gates and angel choirs and happy reunions, not images of globular clusters and spiral galaxies and vast distances. I've wondered how much "outsiders" might be at least slightly confused, if not actually put off by the church's imagery of "heaven." After all, they may suppose, if some church folk deny evolution; perhaps they deny also the existence of all that wonderful panoply of heaven: red giants and white dwarfs, quasars and black holes. Who would want to live in a world without them?

The church's use of "heaven" as a term for God's realm is mostly St. Matthew's fault. In the life of Jesus he wrote, the phrase "Kingdom of Heaven" is regularly used where parallel passages in St. Luke's life of Jesus read "Kingdom of God." Matthew's strong Jewish heritage advised him that the safest way not to take the Holy One's name in vain was not to use it, or synonyms for it, at all. Use "Kingdom of heaven" instead of "Kingdom of God." The problem is that the former phrase conjures up a spatial image of the place which we now know is inhabited by solar winds and stellar dust.

I've wondered if the church's frequent use of the term "heaven' was a contributing factor to my own interest in astronomy, reflected in the next two editorials. The major factor was certainly Dr. McCloskey's Astronomy Club, using a four inch refractor on the black top behind Central High School in Philadelphia during the fifties. My interest was also encouraged in an oblique way by the science fiction novels classmates Lee Auspitz and current health guru Andy Weil and I exchanged. The interest waned during my college days but was strongly rekindled during the Perseid meteor shower by which I was surprised on a beach at Amagansett, Long Island, in 1972. The editorials themselves are expansions of two essays I wrote for "The Observer," the newsletter of the Lehigh Valley Amateur Astronomical Society.

- - - - -

Talking to Strangers
NVD August 14, 2002

Communicating with extraterrestrials has become a popular quest, from the fictional level of close encounter movies or TV shows to the serious business of wide area radio receivers or plaques launched into space with coded information about our planet.

Extraterrestrial communication is, of course, old hat for those of us who talk to a creative Being beyond this time and space or to that being's attendants, the angels or the saints departed. But most of us would probably also enjoy a chance to communicate with other extraterrestrials, in spite of the parental admonition which might be a propos: "don't talk to strangers."

Talking simply with a snail, let alone an extraterrestrial intelligence, would be fascinating. Part of the fascination would be the radical adjustment in perspective it would require in order to understand and be understood.

Common human terms would naturally be lacking in snail vocabulary: walk, jump, run, feet, fingers, hands, ears. Humans, on the other hand, would probably have to learn more than a dozen subtly different snail words for what we refer to with simply one word: "shell". Other adjustments would be needed, as with the term for exuded bodily goo: human "slime" is a negative term; presumably the corresponding snail term is positive. Human concepts, activities, and emotions might seem very strange in a snail's ear . . . or stalk or whatever. And vice versa.

Maybe the only thing in common we'd be able to talk about easily would be the weather. That happens often enough in human conversations.

Conversations with extraterrestrials would be even more fascinating than talking with a snail . . . and even more complicated. In some ways communicating with an alien culture might be like trying to explain to someone blind from birth what sight and vision are like. In that analogy, however, both participants in the conversation are human and have shared backgrounds and presuppositions and perspectives (to use a visual term!).

Radical differences between humans and extraterrestrials might make it an almost overwhelmingly long and tedious task simply to learn one another's vocabularies and grammars, let alone presuppositions and thought patterns.

Assume, for example, that if self-awareness and decision-making ability can arise out of the complex electrical activities coursing around in the circuits of the human brain, then self-awareness and decision-making ability might also arise out of the complex electrical activities coursing through a star. A star might be an extraterrestrial intelligence.

Considering the contrast between the "life-cycle" of a star and a human life cycle, any conversation would need to be carried on by human generation after human generation through centuries, not by a single person in a single day. Also, since it's a safe conjecture that a stars' interests are radically different from humans', the problem arises not just of how we would communicate or how long it would take but of what we would talk about. At least with our own sun, maybe again we'd wind up discussing the weather.

On one level it takes high technology to prepare to communicate with extraterrestrial intelligences: radio arrays that sweep the skies and the rocket-born SETI plaque bearing human images that races through outer space.

(If I could sketch I would do a cartoon: two creatures that look somewhat like dogs, but with the digits of their front paws resembling human hands; one is holding the familiar SETI plaque for the other to look at while the talk balloon says, "They're obviously intelligent, but why would they send us a picture of their pets?")

On another level everyone

can help prepare for communication with extraterrestrial intelligences. Just practice conversations with those whose presuppositions and perspectives are radically different from one's own and try really to understand and make oneself understood. It's not an easy task. But when such aliens as ardent atheists and rigid theologians, ACLU members and rednecks, skinheads and black militants, abortion clinic workers and abortion clinic attackers have learned how to communicate meaningfully across the gulfs that separate them, we'll be better prepared to bridge the vast communication gaps separating us from Martian snails or distant stars.

- - - - -

Talking to Extraterrestrials
NVD September 7, 2002

What will we talk about with extraterrestrials?

Naturally what we talk about with extraterrestrials depends as much on them as it does on our own human interests. Hearing and telling risqué sexual jokes would be out of the question if our correspondents are asexual.

If they're septisexual, how dull and humorless most of our jokes would seem to them. Assuming, of course, that appreciation of humor and awareness of its absence is a trait we share with these aliens. Possibly they'll lack our human capacity for responding to an unexpected incongruity with recognition, affirmation, and pleasure. Even some humans respond to jokes with "I don't get it" or "That doesn't make sense" or "That's not funny."

But imagine being septisexual and NOT having a sense of humor. The human mind boggles.

Presumably, however, we shall burn up the hotlines of interstellar communications with something other than biologically oriented witticisms.

What will we talk about?

The question properly should be divided into two parts. One part, usually overlooked in science fiction about first contacts, is what would we want to tell them about ourselves or about our understandings of things. The other is what would we want to hear or learn from them (or it or whatever pronoun is appropriate).

So much depends on who's working the telestellar teletype. Statements and questions composed by Carl Sagan and fired off to Barnard's star, or a planet around it, would be very different from statements and questions composed by the Dali Lama. Sagan's would surely revolve around cosmic mechanics, and the Dali Lama's would tend to center on cosmological metaphysics.

One of my professors, musing once about how wonderful it would be to discover an extraterrestrial civilization that had a playwright on a par in his/her/their/its civilization with England's Shakespeare, observed with a sigh, "It would be like discovering a whole series of new Shakespeare plays!"

Alas, the kinds of statements and questions used in initial stages of serious transconstellational conferences are not likely to be in the area of literature, English or otherwise. They're more likely to be explorations of unified field theory mathematics and subatomic string harmonics because of the kinds of folk who'll be operating the transmitters.

Microbes meditating on Mimas or bugs orbiting Betelgeuse might even close off transmission with an exasperated, "They're just engineers; all they're interested in is boring technical stuff."

On the other hand, if our first contact is with an alien culture for whom little counts beyond the exploration and discussion of what humans call "hard sciences", we better not put one of our philosophers, theologians, or poets on our end of the line.

Starting with eliminations, we can probably all agree on whom we do NOT want as initial spokespersons: politicians. But given the most likely source of funding for the operation, there's an excellent chance we'll be stuck with major American governmental input into our first superlunar conversational output. Heaven forbid that first contact is in an American election year!

If humanity ever is in fact ready to communicate with aliens, I would hope the first stages would in some way represent not the special interests of scientists, English professors, or congressfolk, all speaking out of an American and western European cultural background, but the general interests and concerns of the whole human race. Achieving consensus on how humanity would start its conversation would be an undertaking more massive than setting up and monitoring radio arrays or propelling metal plaques beyond earth's gravity. And ultimately, even if we never have first contact with extraterrestrials, more helpful.

- - - - -

My address of the interplay between religion and government appeared in the second article in this collection, musing about the wisdom or foolishness of posting the ten, or eleven or twelve commandments on the courthouse wall. I dealt with the same interplay in the following piece musing about a motto that appears on our currency.

- - - - -

In God(s) We Trust

"In God we trust" is a phrase that has always made me uncomfortable, even though I'm a clergy person. My problem with it is that "God" means such different things to different people.

If someone tells me she or he trusts in God and I ask which God, the response is usually, "There is only one!", leaving me without a way to compare the other person's God with the one for whom I'm an officially, though not generously, paid advocate.

"In God I trust" doesn't tell me if the other person's God is a God of mercy who identifies with the underdog, like the one I serve who brought Israel out of Egypt, or a God of power and control who manages everything with a heavy hand and is out, as Maude used to say, to "get you for that". I can't tell if it's a God who gets personally involved in the world or a God who prefers to sit outside the world looking on judgmentally and getting involved only as a disciplinarian, like the one who signed the billboard that says "Don't make me come down there, God".

If "In God we trust" is an official state or federal motto, does it mean the God who is unalterably opposed to abortions on any grounds, or the God who has absolutely no problem with abortions, or the God of most mainline Protestant denominations who straddles the fence?

Conversations get very confusing for me when I'm talking about "God", meaning the one I serve, and the other person is talking about "God", meaning one totally different from mine. It's like having a three person conversation about a "pet" without defining the kinds of pets when my pet is a ninety pound mutt, yours is a parakeet, and the other person's is a three foot alligator. If we assume we're all telling stories and giving advice about the same kind of beast, we're in trouble.

Of course the variation of pets would surface as soon as the alligator owner told us a pet should spend most of its time in water or the parakeet owner asked us if we had problems with our pet flying into mirrors or windows. We'd acknowledge the variety, and no one would say to another, "Oh, but yours isn't really a pet!" The alligator owner might even discover there's something to be said for dogs and I might learn to be more appreciative of parakeets.

People talking about "God", on the other hand, generally refuse to acknowledge that even today Gods, and even Goddesses, are as varied and different as pets. Their assumption seems to be that if the God I'm talking about isn't exactly like the one they're talking about, mine doesn't really exist.

I also get into trouble when people tell me they don't believe in God. I always ask in which God they don't believe. And often what they describe as the God in whom they do not trust bears absolutely no resemblance to the God in whom I do trust. But rather than listen patiently to me describe my God, they impatiently insist that the only proper definition of God is the definition of the one they're sure isn't there.

Ancient pagans were religiously so much more sympathetic than modern folk. They were delightfully willing to admit the possibility of a whole variety of Gods and Goddesses and go on to debate about their relative merits and which was really worth trusting in. Even at the risk of being thrown to the lions for being the advocate of an unpopular God, I'd have found it much more fruitful to live in pagan times.

Back then, in discussions about God we'd know much more clearly each where the other stood when we said "In God we trust". I could argue with an Ephesian silversmith who thinks the only God in which to trust is the virgin huntress Artemis and we could discuss the comparative merits of virginity. Or I could hear from one of Hannibal's soldiers that the only God in which to trust is Baal, who will be pleased only if I sacrifice my firstborn son. And we could compare the meaning of "sacrificing one's son", whether it is metaphorical or literal. It would have been wonderful to try to decide in which God to trust.

But in modern times simply to say "In God we trust" in a society that has such a variety of definitions or understandings of "God" says nothing meaningful.

- - - - -

Steve Corbett of the Wilkes-Barre, Pennsylvania, *Times-Leader*, made some disparaging remark in an editorial about "angels dancing on the head of a pin." From studying medieval literature with Dr. William Kinter and medieval theology with Dr. Hagen Staack as a student at Muhlenberg College I had come to appreciate an era that is often disparagingly dismissed and I hastened in the following piece to the defense of one of its often belittled topics. Originally in the *Times-Leader*, the item reappeared in the *Northern Virginia Daily*.

- - - - -

Angels and Pinheads
NVD September 17, 2002

How many angels can dance on the head of a pin? The question is ridiculed by those who don't appreciate the medieval traditions of theologically sophisticated debates. Scorners disparage the question about how many angels as merely splitting hairs.

Obviously the detractors have never tried to split hairs. It's a very fine and delicate art, exceedingly difficult to do but thoroughly gratifying when it's been accurately accomplished.

How many angels can dance on the head of a pin? The question that seems silly to superficial thinkers has a very serious aspect to those who are willing to join some late medieval philosophers in grappling with the difficulty of defining the relationship between the spiritual and the physical, between the supernatural and the natural.

What is the relationship between non-physical realities and physical realities? That's what is really being asked. Change the terms and it becomes a question asked by twentieth and twenty-first century physicists: How do forces without mass relate with quantifiable masses?

(Substitute "measurable" for "quantifiable". Physicists like to use esoteric terms to add to the mystique of their discipline. Theologians do the same thing. We clergy? Never!)

Modern psychologists as well as physicists, discuss the same angelic question in terms of "the ghost in the machine": How does non-physical self-awareness, consciousness or will, relate with the physical machinery of nerves and sinews and muscles?

People who still believe that humans have a non-physical soul that survives the death of the physical body should take a strong interest in the question of angels interacting with pins. For "angel" substitute "soul" and for "pin" substitute "brain." How does a non-physical soul receive messages from a physical brain? How does a non-physical soul have an effect on a physical brain and move a physical body?

Folk who look forward to chatting with Aunt Tillie or Uncle Ned at a seance – I don't believe in it myself – also have a serious stake in that old medieval question. Non-physical beings, in this case ghosts or spirits rather than angels, are supposed to be knocking on the table or vibrating air molecules to cause sound rather than tiptoeing on the pinhead. But it's the same principle, and if the seance-goers could explain how angels can dance on the head of a pin, they could make me a believer in the possibility of a ghost wrapping on a table at a seance or manipulating the planchette of a Ouija Board.

Even if the question about angels and pins is no longer popular but still used to disparage medieval metaphysics, at least angels themselves have regained a popularity that for a few generations they had lost.

Fortunately, as far as I'm concerned as a Christian clergy-person, angels have become popular once again through books and magazine articles and cards and television programs.

Unfortunately, as far as I'm concerned as a close reader of the Bible and a student of the church's long tradition, the popular presentation of angels is just plain wrong.

Serious scripture readers know better than to present angels as the kind of pudgy little winged babies that are popular on notecards and wrapping paper; angels are overwhelmingly awesome beings. The first thing they must always say as their beholders fall to the ground before their majesty is "Fear not!" And medieval theologians knew there was a distinction between the powerful, transcendent angels, who were created at the dawn of time, and the souls of some departed Jane-or-Johnny-come-lately like those who wind up doing extra time on earth in our contemporary movies and television shows claiming to be about angels.

Whether dancing on pins or not, angels have come to be accepted in our society only by being trivialized, just as the very serious metaphysical question about angels has been trivialized. Our society does not want to confront the transcendent, powerful, and awesome Others any more than it wants to wrestle with the rough metaphysical questions of how spiritual realities relate to physical realities.

What puzzles me is not how many angels can dance on the head of a pin but rather why so many pinheads dance frivolously around the question of angels.

- - - - -

Steve Corbett of the *Times-Leader* in Wilkes-Barre, Pennsylvania, also made a reference to the damage done by "organized religion," with the lurking implication that religions are much better off if they're disorganized. My response, which appeared not as an editorial but as a letter to the editor, tried to reassure him that Lutherans and most of the religions I know are really not well organized. I later adapted the letter as the following editorial for the *Northern Virginia Daily*. Since then I can add another example of our bureaucratic disorganization. I mailed a copy of my editorials to Mark Hansen, the presiding bishop of the Evangelical Lutheran Church in America, with a request that he write a few words about them that I could use for publicity. He wrote back that he didn't provide endorsements but he very much enjoyed reading my hymns! Trying to put a charitable construction on his response, I tell myself he must have been very impressed by the lyrical and poetic quality of my essays. In skeptical moods I assume his error was just another example of disorganization in the upper levels of religious management.

- - - - -

Disorganized Religion
NVD October 11, 2002

Organized religion often receives blame for the world's woes and wars, insolence and ignorance, prejudices and persecutions.

People who blame "organized religion" for those kinds of problems should consider joining the denomination of which I'm a pastor. We're definitely not an organized religion. In fact, we Lutherans are a very disorganized religion.

Consider...

How disorganized would a football team be in which only one third of the players show up for regular practice? Or a dramatic group where only one third of the cast come out for regular rehearsals? Those are the national denominational statistics for the team I'm called to coach, the cast I'm supposed to direct: only one third of those officially signed on show up each week. And national statistics for most other denominations are about the same. Organizations hardly well organized.

Organized or disorganized? Consider communications I've received from the office of my religious superiors. One letter had a paragraph that ended incomprehensibly in the middle of a sentence; another told me to share greetings with St. Mark's (I was serving St. John's at the time); another assured me that an application I never submitted for a position I knew nothing about had been forwarded to a church I had never heard of.

Organized religion? Not us!

Now that's just my denomination. But come to think of it, how many Christian denominations are there? All of us disagreeing with one another, conflicting and competing with one another. Is it fair to call Christianity an organized religion? Hardly.

Once I was so concerned about Christianity's disorganization I called a rabbi friend of mine, figuring his folk had been around millennia longer than mine and therefore must have excellent organizational skills.

He said of course he had time to chat because the wedding he was getting ready to do had been scheduled to start only ten minutes before I called. Perturbed by his own seeming lack of organizational skills, I nonetheless told him I was depressed because Christianity was disorganized into so many different camps and I asked the secret of Judaism's uniformity. He went on and on about Hasidim and conservatives and Ashkenazim and reconstructionists and Zionists and orthodox and Sephardim . . .

Aware he still had a wedding to perform, I interrupted to ask what superior organizational skills Judaism had that kept it around so long.

By the time he finally stopped laughing he really did have to go in and start the wedding and I didn't get an answer.

Several days later the rabbi called me back to report that he had shared my question with four colleagues and among the five of them they came up with seven possible answers but couldn't agree on any of them and would keep on discussing it.

I began to rethink my impression that Judaism is one of the organized religion.

Probably if the religions of Moses and Jesus really were in fact organized there wouldn't be the kinds of damage the detractors refer to: prejudice and pogroms, presumption and profiteering, "holy" wars and slaughter. Religions, if they were really organized, could work strenuously and effectively for the ideals and goals promulgated by their founders: mercy and justice, healing and hope, reconciliation and renewal.

Maybe the problem isn't organized religion. Maybe the damage is really done by disorganized religion.

- - - - -

Since the fear among some church folk that Hallowe'en practices play right into Satan's hands and therefore should be shunned has always irritated me, I addressed it in the following editorial and refer to it again in a Christmas editorial further down the line. The first part of this editorial is an abridged form of a dramatic first person monologue I had developed for a congregation's Hallowe'en party back before any congregations became antsy about sponsoring them.

- - - - -

The Ghostly Holiday Approaches
NVD October 2002

Late October. Leaves turn brown and fall. Vegetation dies. Darkness begins earlier every evening. The air turns chilly. Against winter's onset in our village we huddle around our cottage hearth for warmth and companionship.

Late October. Huddled, chatting, we mention family members who used to gather around the fire with us but who have died. We wonder what has become of them in death. We ask if their restless spirits remember the warmth and love around our hearth and in autumn's chill want to gather with us once again.

Late October. In early darkness beyond our cottage window, a rustling noise. The gathering of the grim and lonely spirits of the dead? Or just the wind in the dry leaves and harvest stubble? Noises on the roof. Some dreadful haunt seeking entry? Or just the tap of a tree branch or settling of the thatch?

Late October. And if the gruesome ghosts of those long gone are gathering once again, what can we do? Perhaps frighten them away with a fearsome face carved in a gourd and left in a window. Perhaps appease them with gifts of fruit or cakes left outside the door as sign of good will and in hope the gruesome horrors do not come inside. Trick them or treat them. Or both.

Late October now brings Hallowe'en, All Hallows Evening, the festival with which the Church once tried, not very successfully, to replace the autumnal pagan fears and rites. Instead of warding off the dreaded dead by tricks or treats, the Church's folk were encouraged to remember the departed, all the hallowed ones, not with fear or appeasement, but with thanksgiving and confidence.

Late October, and old habits die hard. Not nearly so many attend the Church's remembrances on All Saints Day as reenact with variations the practices of the pagan past. The carved gourd still watches out the window, though in the New World it's more often a pumpkin, and it grins as often as it grimaces.

Appeasement with little goodies at the door continues, though not for real ghosts but merely for children in costume, role playing the ancient ritual in the most common and basic hallowe'en costume, the sheet. But now, of course, with those sheeted ghosts appear other weird creatures: Mutant Ninja Turtles and Power Ranger, Lion Kings and Indian Princesses.

Fear of the dead evolved indeed a darker side: Appeasement of the ghostly legions not just by cakes and fruit, but by alliances with the powers of the underworld, by witchery and necromancy, by vile worship and evil sacrifice.

But it is not from that dark side that our grimacing pumpkins and trick-or-treaters descend. They are remnants, rather, of a more naive and in some ways innocent practice. And their very parody of fears no longer held reminds us in a playful way of how far we've come.

Written before the film version of Tolkien's *The Fellowship of the Ring* won academy awards and Harry Potter became popular, the following is a reflection on the place of fantasy literature in the modern world.

Frodo and Fantasies
NVD November 13, 2002

Dungeons and dragons? Well, I like the dragons part; dungeons I try to avoid. Wizards and witches? The picture of Gandolf confronting a Balrog on the stone bridge at Khaza Dum enthralls me; I'm disappointed by a simpering divorcee who laments that her rediscovered coven of ancient goodwomen has always been tragically misunderstood.

Fantasy stuff, which has

made a come-back in American culture, gets a mixed reaction out of me as a clergy person. In some ways I'm glad; in other ways I'm disappointed.

Since the enlightenment several centuries ago educated and rationalistic Western civilization refused to take seriously the reality of the spiritual, miraculous, and magical. Hard evidence and scientific proof were all the rage.

During that period in intellectual circles Christianity came to be either despised as superstition or stripped of spiritual realities like angels and demons or of miraculous realities like physical healing and forgiveness of sins or of magical realities like water that gives new life and bread and wine that nourish eternal life.

Church and culture for a while seemed to be playing by different rules. One claimed to rely strictly on natural standards interpreted by scientific methods, the other introduced the supernatural accepted by experience and trust. As if society had been playing football and we in the Church were playing basketball and lost the ball every time we tried to dribble. But now basketball is on the rebound and the Church should be able to score points.

Fantasy, which includes the miraculous and magical, has become much more acceptable in our society than it used to be.

Fantasy literature, with its offspring of fantasy games like dungeons and dragons, has become popular enough to take over large sections of shelf space in book stores where, thirty years ago, it wasn't even a category. People enjoy reading about the magical and miraculous, and watching it on television, and playing games with it, much more than they used to.

Today's fantasy literatures actually descend from two very committed Christian writers: J. R. R. Tolkien and C. S. Lewis, whose pretend worlds of Middle-Earth and Narnia were imaginary counterparts of what they believed were the real world of angels and devils, spirits and sacraments.

It's as if some angel had whispered in Tolkien's and Lewis's ears: "Create a pretend world to show modern folk they can believe in the mysterious and supernatural once again." And then some devil, a cousin perhaps of Lewis's Screwtape, whispered to a whole host of writers, "Create an abundance of pretend worlds so that people will be so fascinated by them they won't investigate the real supernatural world."

With the popularity of fantasy in today's world has come also the popularity of much for which the older enlightenment culture had little time or interest. With literal acceptance of fantasy today comes also belief in and practice of magic, wizardry and witchcraft, the use of gems, oils, and incantations.

Literary or literal, the renaissance of fantasy on the one hand discourages me: it misdirects too much energy, as far as I'm concerned, to inconsequential ends. On the other hand it encourages me: it proves people are very hungry indeed for more than the scientifically provable.

Folks nowadays who are willing to suspend disbelief in order to play a game involving dragons may come to be willing to believe in St. George. Those open to believing in the mystical qualities of a coven may become open to believing in the mystical qualities of a convent. Those who use esoteric oils or incantations may decide to try the Church's anointings or say a proper barucha before the meal.

Much of the modern involvement with fantasy is simply a wishful game of "Let's pretend." But playing the game of "Let's pretend" can lead to the more serious business – the business I'm in as a clergyperson – of Make Believe.

- - - - -

The following editorial is a more formal presentation of some ideas I bounced around informally with a Bible study group at one of the congregations I served. That discussion also included comments about the style of prayer that helped produce the subsequent article.

The Limits of Prayer
NVD November 22, 2002

Congregations I've served and I are often on different wavelengths. They regularly confess to me, though not in the formal sense, that they believe in the Power of Prayer. And I must confess, in the formal sense, that I do not.

My skepticism about the power of prayer obviously puts me out of touch with modern society, which seems to be having a renaissance of belief in things like prayer and angels. I've become an antiquated fossil – many people think clergy have always been antiquated fossils – because I don't shout Amen to the wealth of material in magazines and on television about the power of prayer. Newsweek had a cover story "The Mystery of Prayer." I was glad the title was "The Mystery" and not "The Power of Prayer," because, quite frankly, I don't think prayer "works". Don't tell my bishop. But if you do tell him, please explain to him exactly what I mean . . .

I certainly believe in the Power of God. God has power to do all kinds of things: kindle galaxies, design DNA, supervise evolution, forgive sins, heal illness, still storms, grant peace, and make house-plants grow faster.

And I certainly believe that God hears our prayers and is responsive to them: sometimes responding positively, sometimes negatively, sometimes strangely or obliquely.

But it is not Prayer that has the Power; it is God that has the Power, including the power of saying "not yet" or even "not at all!" to our prayers, no matter how many are praying and no matter how fervently. So it is not Prayer that "works", it is God who works if God so chooses.

Sunday School, which in some ways was more effective for me than the seminaries I've attended, taught me, and I still firmly believe, that "Prayer is conversation with God". My expectations of prayer are consequently the same as my expectations of conversation. I do not believe in "The Power of Conversation" in the same way in which many of my congregants believe in "The Power of Prayer."

Prayer and conversation do indeed have power to deepen understanding, to enrich relationships, and even – sometimes – to get things accomplished. But just as saying to a spouse or offspring, "Please bring me a soda" or "Please wash the dishes" or "I wish you'd stop dating that clown" – no matter how often, strongly, sweetly, persuasively, argumentatively, trustingly, or demandingly said – doesn't have the infallible power to put a soda in our hands or get the dishes washed or terminate an unwelcome relationship, so too our requests of God do not always wind up with the changes we may be asking for. In the sense, then, of getting what we want accomplished, conversation and prayer do not always "work".

My bishop's prayers, in the popular sense in which folk talk about the power of prayer, do not work. I have often heard him in solemn assembly, with mitre, crozier, chasuble, and microphone, pray eloquently and lengthily for world peace, and a thousand of us in attendance have regularly responded with a resounding "Amen" – or as resounding an amen as you can expect from bashful German Lutherans. And the next day the newspapers report not peace but the outbreak of some new aspect of warfare.

Probably it's a reasonably fair exchange. God asks us to be caring and concerned, just and generous with one another, and we don't always do as we're asked. We ask God for peace or healing or justice or nice weather for the wedding and God doesn't always give what we want.

About the power of prayer my congregation says one thing; I say something else. The important thing is that we keep talking, deepening our relationship by continuing our communicating and increasing our understanding of one another.

Maybe in that sense prayer – our conversations with God – does have power and does in fact work.

- - - - -

As above, I often advise my readers, "Don't tell my bishop," as if my bishops were harshly authoritarian figures who relentlessly demanded that I toe a Lutheran doctrinal party-line with no doubts, no challenges, and no hesitation. My actual intention was to give my opinions an aura of unconventionality, which is in some cases appropriate. But I hope the repeated phrase is not taken seriously as a depiction of the Lutheran Church and especially of its leaders as inflexible and monolithic. At times indeed they can be. But more often they allow – sometimes even encourage – the kinds of questioning and challenging and rethinking that occur in many of my essays.

For my representation, then, of my bishops as stern taskmasters to be feared, I consequently apologize. Most, although not all, of the bishops under whom I have served as my interim ministries took me through various jurisdictions have been flexible and understanding, patient and supportive, especially Harold Weiss and David Strobel in

Northeastern Pennsylvania Synod, and Roy Almquist in Southeastern Pennsylvania.

- - - - -

Plain Talk with God
NVD December 11, 2002

Churches have made it difficult, I am convinced as a clergyperson, for people to offer meaningful public prayers. Unfortunate folk in the pews, whether construction workers or Ph.D.s, have an almost impossible standard set for them when they hear their clergy converse with the Deity.

In fact, most clergy don't set an example of conversing, because conversation involves a back and forth give and take. Most clergy deliver a monologue.

My own Lutheran tradition has very ornate monologues, even when very brief: "Almighty and most merciful God, thou who dost cause precipitation to descend upon both the just and unjust, vouchsafe to open the vaults of heaven etc. etc."

Normal people, a category which obviously excludes us clergy, would not talk that way. They would say, "Lord, please send rain!"

Verbs like "vouchsafe" or archaic forms like "thou" and "dost" make church prayers an arcane language. Of course, give credit: some churches are updating their language. Instead of "omniscient", for example, they say "all-knowing." (When's the last time you heard someone say "all-knowing?")

Friends in traditions not as formal as mine claim their prayers do not include those rhetorical flourishes and linguistic blandishments but are just natural speech.

Wrong. Their prayers simply have a different kind of artificiality.

Although those friends <u>never</u> use "just" as part of their normal speech patterns, they have it popping up all through their prayers: "Father-God, we just want to thank you . . . it's just wonderful . . . we just ask you to just give our sister just a touch of your healing power."

Likewise, when we talk theology, these same friends say "Jesus" the same normal way I do. But there's something about that name when they say it in public prayer: a noticable "ch" sound is part of the J, and the E sound drags out for three times its normal length and often lilts. Their clergy, like ours, are probably to blame for setting a prayer pattern not resembling regular and normal speech habits.

Another unfortunate example of clergy misguiding our praying flocks is our occasional use of prayer to deliver information to the congregation. Some clergy, for example, repeat the three main points of the sermon, prefacing them with, in my tradition, something like "Omniscient Potentate, thou art fully cogniscent of the fact that . . .", or, in other traditions, "Good God, you just know that . . ."

Personally I gave up working sermon points into my prayers because in the midst – I mean in the middle – of praying I sometimes forgot what my third point had been and I dreaded the congregation thinking I hadn't paid as much attention to my sermon as I had expected them to.

From us, people have learned to use their public prayers not to address the Deity but to sneak a message to the congregation. The Ladies Aid president prays aloud, "Lord, we just want to thank you for our women's luncheon that's going to be this coming Wednesday at noon. We just want as many ladies to come to it as can. Lord, you just know that everybody's welcome."

Just dreadful.

Figuring my Jewish sisters and brothers – cousins? – practiced prayer longer than any of us in the Christian tradition, I called my rabbi friend and asked if I could sit in on his morning prayer service.

Graciously welcomed, I heard their prayers begin: Y'isgadosh v'yisgadol . . . and continue on incomprehensibly.

Talk about not using the language of every-day life! I asked him how they had managed to survive as long as they had.

"It hasn't been easy, considering some of the things we've had to deal with," he commented, shooting me an accusing look. "Only by the grace of God."

Actually I had known that. I also suspected God pays extra attention to prayers in Hebrew. Extra attention is necessary to understand it!

Church prayers or Hebrew prayers, I insist, whether polysyllabic pontifications or just homely chats, encourage people to think there's a particular language or style that has to be used to make the prayer official, and as a result their public prayers become very stilted, artificial, and unreal.

Private prayers fortunately remain real. One of my deacons was very adept at public prayer, using "supplication" instead of "request" and "grant" instead of "give". Until his son was in a serious automobile accident and we prayed together. Our Creator didn't hear that my friend was "fraught with excessive ire because of the untoward circumstances besetting him behind and before." My friend told our Creator up front that he was "p-----d off about the s--t that's been dumped on me and sure as h--- want my son to get better." No lightning bolt and, in fact, his son did get better.

That's the realistic style just once in my career I'd like to use in public prayer at the altar. Maybe right before I retire. Don't tell my bishop.

- - - - -

The following Christmas story, purely fictional, inspired a young man from St. Mark, Mechanicsburg, to buy me a package of bottle rockets in the hope we could bring the fantasy to life. We didn't try. Yet. Maybe some day, some sweet day . . .

First Christmas Eve: No 'Silent Night'
NVD December 16, 2002

Yuletide always reminds me of the time my devotion to the Bible earned me a special Christmas surprise from my bishop: relocation to a new parish.

Normally I don't pay close attention to the hymns my congregations sing, but it was a few weeks before Christmas and the Worship Committee had scheduled "It came upon a Midnight Clear." I thought how some of my clergy colleagues would shudder to be singing Christmas carols weeks before Christmas and I noticed something strange about the carol: There is no reference at all to Jesus or to Jesus' birth.

So I paid closer attention the next Sunday, for which the Worship Committee had chosen

"The First Noel." I found myself singing about shepherds "Who looked up And saw a star Shining in the East Beyond them far."

Wait a minute, I thought. St. Luke says nothing about the shepherds seeing or following a star. They had a message from angels and instead of following a star they had to go from door to door tracking down the sign the angels gave: a babe wrapped in swaddling cloths lying in a food trough.

Lo, Christmas Eve was hastening on and I thought I'd better check the accuracy of our hymns for such a major festival. The Worship Committee had chosen as the special hymn of the evening, to be accompanied by the solemnity of candlelighting, the perennial Christmas Eve favorite of Lutherans and Catholics, Baptists and Episcopalians: Silent Night.

I read it. "Silent night . . . All is calm . . . Sleep in heavenly peace". I thought about it. I reread it.

Whatever Joseph Mohr may have been experiencing when he wrote the hymn while traveling by sleigh through the snow hushed hills of Oberndorf, the hymn is not true to the Biblical account of the first Christmas eve.

Christmas eve was hardly a "silent night". Nor was it calm. Sleeping would have been impossible. Childbirth tends to be noisy. A multitude of singing heavenly host tend to be noisy. Shepherds banging on doors trying to find a babe wrapped in swaddling cloths tend to be noisy. No record survives of Joseph's comments when his exhausted wife and he were disturbed by strange and coarse shepherds yelling to one another "Here he is, here he is" after their noisy search through Bethlehem. But I bet Joseph's remarks were equally coarse and equally noisy.

Of course the hymn does ring true for the Christmas eve crowd who sing it and then, as far as church involvement goes, sleep until Easter. Maybe that's why it's so popular. But it's definitely not Biblical.

Unfortunately St. Matthew and St. Luke have made less of an impression on our images of Christmas than Hallmark has.

One year with the help of a youth group I created a special worship experience during our Christmas eve service, which for many years had been held at 8:30 p.m. but was still known as "the midnight service."

Surprise was a major feature of the first Christmas. Mary

was surprised to hear from an angel that she was pregnant. Joseph and she were surprised by a census that required their relocation to Bethlehem. The shepherds in the fields were surprised by a celestial sound-and-light spectacular overhead.

So surprise was what the youth and I provided the congregation. As worshippers slowly and piously slushed through "Silent Night", one lad threw the circuit breaker on the organ, which sighed into silence. A young lady brought up Bach's "Break Forth, Oh Beauteous Heavenly Light" to full volume on her boom box. The high intensity strobe light concealed in the hay of the creche was turned on. Young folk set off Roman candles outside each window. And a handful of my youth group's finest fired a bevy of bottle rockets from the balcony over the heads of the congregation.

You think the shepherds in the dark fields were surprised? You should have seen the congregation!

The following year some of the youth wrote me to volunteer their help doing a Christmas eve service in the new congregation to which I had been assigned. I thanked them but replied that I had decided that, as was true of the first Christmas, once was enough.

- - - - -

Having first appeared in Wilkes-Barre's *Times-Leader* in the mid nineties, the following editorial has been printed in a variety of newspapers. I submit editorials wherever my interim ministry may lead me. Most are declined. Holiday pieces are occasionally accepted. This one has appeared most widely.

- - - - -

𝕷ate for 𝕮hristmas
𝔑𝔙𝔇 𝔇ecember 18, 2002

Last minute Christmas shoppers like me have very special patron and matron saints: Joseph and Mary, the parents of the baby whose birth, believe it or not, is what Christmas celebrates.

Going from store to store, from counter to counter, and hearing again and again from the salesfolk, "We ran out of that item weeks ago!", I console myself by remembering Mary and Joseph going from inn to inn and hearing again and again, "Sorry, sir and madam, we ran out of rooms weeks ago!" And as I wonder as I wander from store to store, instead of vowing to start earlier the next year I simply enjoy the saintly company I wander with.

Preparing early for Christmas is very important to some people. In fact, some stores start preparing so early that they provoke their customers: "I can't find the Fourth of July decorations with all these Christmas displays standing around!" Most stores, however, don't begin their preparations until Labor Day. Or just a little bit before.

Many of my clergy colleagues are also obsessed with the idea of spending time to prepare for Christmas. They write scathing articles in their church newsletters and argue vehemently with their worship planning committees that Christmas carols should not be sung nor trees set up until December 24. The four weeks before Christmas, they vociferously insist, should be a time of preparation.

Preparing for Christmas has never been high on my agenda. I don't start preparing, as the stores do, at Hallowe'en. I don't start preparing, as my clergy colleagues encourage, during the four Sundays of Advent. I always find it very easy to ignore Christmas preparations altogether until around December 23.

Then suddenly I notice something. Santa Claus ringing a Salvation Army bell outside the supermarket. Or my congregation singing "It came upon a Midnight Clear" in broad daylight. And I'm startled by the realization: Christmas is in just two days. (Mary, Joseph, lend your aid; I'm off to the stores!)

Preparations, whether from Labor Day on or only for four weeks of Advent season, are in no way appropriate for Christmas. The good news of Christmas – I wouldn't dare preach this to a congregation who's been obsessed with shopping and decorating and lighting an Advent wreathe – is that even when things happen that we're not prepared for or expecting, we're given the strength to take them in stride and make a good response.

Mary's baby wasn't planned and prepared for; she

was simply told "Surprise! You're pregnant!" She managed. There was no preparation of cribs and purchase of cute little outfits; Joseph and Mary at the last minute made do with a feeding trough and left-over gunny sack. They managed. Shepherds didn't have weeks, or even days, to look forward to taking time off from work, dress in their finest, and go to visit the Infant. Christmas night was there before the shepherds knew it! As soon as they heard the news, off they went, totally unprepared and not even sure where they were going. But they managed.

We who are late preparers for Christmas often engender in others a scornful disbelief: "What?! You haven't done your shopping yet? I don't believe it. What?! You're not using the four Sundays of Advent as solemn preparation? I don't believe it."

We ignore the scorn and disbelief. We know we're the only ones who, with Mary and Joseph and the shepherds, celebrate Christmas the way it really was and really should be.

- - - - -

Maybe it was the Jewish-Christian mix at Central High School that gave me an ecumenical spirit. Wherever it came from, it has always made me sympathetic to the Week of Prayer for Christian Unity, as described in the following.

- - - - -

A Time to Bridge Denominational Differences
NVD January 18, 2003

"We're getting like Roman Catholics" some Protestant church folk complained when their minister adopted new robes for worship or their congregation voted for more frequent Holy Communion services.

"We're turning into Protestants," complained many Roman Catholics after Vatican 2 in the sixties replaced the Latin Mass with English, encouraged more hymn singing, and even put hymnals in the pews with "A Mighty Fortress" by Martin Luther.

January 18 to January 25, observed by both the Roman Catholic Church and by most Protestant churches as "The Week of Prayer for Christian Unity," is a good time to reflect on differences and similarities.

Theological differences naturally exist among the variety of expressions of the Christian faith, but more obvious to the people in the pew are differences in practice.

For example, when church folk like Presbyterians or Disciples of Christ who are used to having the bread and cup distributed in the pews see Lutherans or Episcopalians going forward to receive Communion, their first reaction is often "How strange and different." Perhaps a better, second reaction would be "But after all, they're doing the same thing we do, obeying Jesus' command; it's only their delivery system that's different."

In many basic ways the variety of Christian denominations share deep and important similarities. They believe the same Bible and read from it every Sunday, often even the same set of lessons. They baptize "in the name of the Father and of the Son and of the Holy Spirit". They acknowledge the Apostles' Creed as a basic statement of core beliefs: God created everything; God's Son came, died, rose, and will come again; God's Spirit works through God's people to give forgiveness and new life. And they all take very seriously Jesus' command "Do this in remembrance of me."

Similarities are so obvious, however, that they can too easily be taken for granted and then overlooked in the face of obvious differences.

Sensitive Christians of whatever brand, encountering differences, ask themselves "How important is this difference? Is it really significant?"

Should handclapping during worship really be a cause of offense to someone from a less boisterously noisy a tradition? Should a worship leader in elaborate vestments be a cause of offense to someone used to a worship leader in a suit and tie?

Some differences, like how the bread and cup are shared, how the worship leader is garbed, what style of music is sung, are really inconsequential, more matters of taste than of theology. Similarly some differences are more a matter of terminology than of principle. Call it Eucharist, Mass, Holy Communion, the Lord's Supper, or Divine Liturgy, it's the reception of bread and the fruit of the vine obeying Jesus' command, "This do . . .", and trusting Jesus' promise, "This is . . ."

Of course there are serious theological differences. All who obey the command "This do" do not agree on how the sharing of bread and wine works as a means of grace. Debating the differences can lead to spirited disagreements. But it's to be hoped that the spirit of those disagreements is the Spirit of humility and patience, not a spirit of self-righteousness and animosity.

Amid the variety of those who confess Jesus as Savour some baptize candidates by immersion when they're old enough to respond; some baptize babies by sprinkling; some in the Eastern Orthodox traditions baptize babies by immersion. Biblical and theological differences lie behind the varied practices, but all agree baptism is Jesus' commanded way for a person to become part of God's family.

Some may think others are doing baptisms wrong, but at least all are doing them. They need also to be listening to one another, trying to understand one another and be patient with one anothers' misunderstandings and errors. The real question is not "Why can't those other Christians do it right?" The real question is "Can I understand their reasons for being different and love them anyway, even if I cannot accept those reasons?"

Encountering denominational differences, children of God take them not as excuses for quarreling but as opportunities for dialogue.

The Week of Prayer for Christian Unity took its scriptural beginning from Jesus' prayer in John 17:21 that his disciples "might be one." His language echoed marriage language, "The two shall become one" (Matthew 19:5). As marital unity does not mean uniformity – male and female remain separate and different – but unanimity of goal and purpose in spite of the separateness and differences, so too church unity need not mean uniformity of practice or even of belief but does imply unanimity of goal and purpose, being God's forgiven people working together to heal the world's brokenness.

- - - - -

"What would Jesus do?" became a popular enough ethical question in 2002 that WWJD appeared on bumper sticker, lapel pins, refrigerator magnets, and teenagers' bracelets. As SUVs became popular a variation of the question, "What would Jesus drive?" was asked by a nationally syndicated columnist. Although I'm not (yet) syndicated, I responded.

- - - - -

Jesus Drives . . . A Hard Bargain
NVD January 23, 2003

"What Would Jesus Drive?", for all its recent popularity, might in fact be a bogus question. It assumes that Jesus would have some kind of gasoline powered vehicle as the rest of us do. And that's a very questionable assumption because the clear Biblical witness is that Jesus steadfastly refused to be like the rest of us.

Is there any reason, other than wanting Jesus to seem like the rest of us, to believe Jesus would drive anything? During the period of his ministry he was content to walk. He had neither horse nor donkey, neither chariot nor cart. He was never, according to the Bible, carried aloft in a sedan chair borne by the shoulders of six disciples. Why assume he would drive a car at all?

The only occasion when Jesus rode anything, according to all four official accounts of his life, it was a borrowed donkey (Mark 11:1-10). Is that the equivalent of a rent-a-car? Or a short term lease? Or borrowing a vehicle from a friend?

And, for our further guidance, are there any other situations which merit a ride than an entry into Jerusalem for Passover?

Of course you could include Jesus' riding a cloud into heaven (Acts 1:9). But then you'd have to take into consideration the Church's clear distinction between the earthly Jesus and the resurrected Christ.

There are other variants of the question "What Would Jesus Do?" beyond "What Would Jesus Drive?"

What Would Jesus Do for someone facing a legal death sentence? Unlike what the rest of us are likely to do, Jesus dismissed a woman clearly guilty of a capital crime with the simple command, "Don't do it again" (John 10:1-11).

And unlike what the rest of us would probably do, even when he himself had been victimized, mugged by the official power structure, and subjected to imminent and undeserved death, he called not for retribution against his persecutors, not even for their rehabilitation, but for their forgiveness. Tell it to Al Sharpton.

Trying to guess Jesus' choice of a car is certainly a much safer moral exercise for us than trying to imitate his lifestyle, or deathstyle, to both of which we have ample witnesses.

What Would Jesus Do about a place to live? Suburbs or inner-city? Rural retreat or ghetto apartment? Condo or cottage? The clear Biblical witness is that Jesus, unlike the rest of us, never encumbered himself with a permanent dwelling. As an itinerant preacher, a wandering Jew, he declared to those who wanted to follow him that although foxes had burrows and birds had nests, he himself had no place to lay his head (Matthew 8:20). Presumably neither would those who followed him.

What Would Jesus Do with the television remote? Watch reality shows to get a clear perspective on how sick the taste of many Americans has become? Or news shows? Sitcoms or quiz shows? Sports events or dramas? Or, in the same mood in which he expressed his disgust at the greed of the traders in the Temple (John 2:13-16), would he crack and grind the remote under his heel?

What Would Jesus Do about helping an offspring choose the right college? What Would Jesus Do about campaigning for a political candidate who insisted on prayer in the public school but also favored abortions on demand? What Would Jesus Do facing a decision about terminating a loved one on a life support system?

Aren't those really unfair questions to ask of one whom we know through the Bible only as a simple, first century Jewish rabbi who never said anything about today's complex systems of higher education and probably never went to formal school himself, who was unfamiliar with modern political structures and problems and never had a chance to vote himself, or who was a total stranger to current medical possibilities and procedures?

Of course the Church's developed theology of the Trinity speaks of Jesus as in some ways more than just an Aramaic speaking carpenter's son with probably no education. It claims that in some ways Jesus is an equal with or the same as or a manifestation of the Eternal, uncreated God.

But then the question goes beyond Jesus, the Word made flesh, and addresses the eternal Word in its existence beyond the limitations of flesh restricted by time and space. It's no longer What Would Jesus Do? What would an itinerant Jewish preacher living in the Roman province of Syria during Tiberius' emperorship do? Rather the question becomes What would the transcendent, creative power of God have us do? What Would God Want Us to Drive? And the perspective from which we address that question is much broader than the four gospel accounts of Jesus' sojourn in Palestine.

What Would Jesus Drive? According to the Bible, the only important driving we need to know about Jesus doing is this: Jesus would drive people to reconsider their values and reevaluate their priorities, to work harder at being generous and gracious, caring and helpful, just and merciful.

- - - - -

One of the *Northern Virginia Daily's* staff writers had written a piece about church attendance. I didn't think numbers were important; quality rather than quantity is my approach. So I responded. The laudable fairness and even-handedness of the *Daily*'s editor, John Horan, are evident in his willingness to print an editorial that implicitly criticizes one of his staff.

- - - - -

Church is More Than Sunday
NVD February 7, 2003

Church attendance statistics, the number of people gathering for worship, although always popular as a newspaper item, are really neither so important nor significant as the number of people actively being the church wherever they are on Monday, Tuesday, or the rest of the week.

Keeping count and tallying statistics are recent emphases resulting from the stress on scientific methodology that began a few centuries ago in the "Enlightenment". The presupposition is that something counts only if it's countable and nothing doesn't measure up if you can't measure it.

"Church goers" accomplished most not in large numbers but when they were a very small percentage of a hostile society, the Roman Empire. Actually they didn't even "go to church"; there were no churches. They gathered in very small groups in one another's houses. Yet this tiny minority was powerful enough to help topple longstanding beliefs in ancient gods and goddesses and to change society completely.

Towards the end of the first century Pliny, governor of Asia Minor, in a surviving letter to the Roman emperor Trajan, reported that Christians got together before dawn – the Roman calendar didn't have a seven day week with one day off – pledged to keep the commandments, to sang a hymn, and shared some food before going off to work. Pliny adds that there hadn't been many to begin with and their numbers had declined when investigations had started.

Small in numbers, they nonetheless survived and thrived.

Large numbers of fourth century Romans increased the Christian census after the emperor Constantine gave the church special status. The huge church basilicas he built were better adapted for mass spectacles than for the close-knit intimacy of house fellowship meetings. Presumably many folk thronged those vast halls not so much to hear about Jesus as to catch a distant glimpse of the emperor himself entering in imperial pomp and ceremony with the colorful panoply of attendants and incense, banners and fasci.

Worship services at that time were well attended; statistics were way up. But how much impact did it make? For many people the faith was a fad and there's a question how deeply commitment ran and how much of people's involvement was simply being stylish. Then, as now, it's easier to count heads than what's in the heads.

In the Middle Ages Christianity as the religion of the majority in Europe did good things and had a helpful impact on society at large with works of charity and mercy, the use of abbeys and monasteries, deaneries and cathedrals, for hospitals, hospices for travelers, and orphanages.

But at the same time many blatantly behaved in ways Jesus wouldn't approve. Even leaders engaged in ecclesiastical nepotism, assigning lucrative posts to nephews or even their own illegitimate offspring. They did wheeling and dealing in large tracts of property. They mounted the crusades, devastating Jewish communities in Europe to warm up for conquest of Muslims in the near east. They provided ample ammunition for people who like to write letters to the editor about the dreadful effects of religion.

These moral problems between eight hundred and fourteen hundred were possible primarily because the church had become so politically powerful by being so pervasive in the population.

To Jesus himself numbers of followers seemed not to matter much. When he sent out his disciples he didn't tell them to bring together as many as possible to sing hymns and say prayers and reflect on Scripture. He didn't send his followers out to recruit; he told them to serve society, to announce that the Creator-God of Israel was nearby and involved, and to serve those in need (Matt. 10:5 ff.).

In fact, Jesus himself actually discouraged some folk from following him by setting the standards of discipleship too high for them (Luke 9:57 ff.). And those who did follow him he called "the salt of the earth" and "leaven in the loaf" (Matt. 5:13; 13:33). Both metaphors imply a tiny amount that does a lot of work, a small but active group having a preservative or flavoring effect on human culture or a leavening effect.

After Jesus' departure his followers continued meeting regularly to keep his spirit alive by retelling the Story and sharing his adaptation of the Passover meal. But the main purpose of these get togethers was to equip and enable them to witness and serve in their daily lives; worship wasn't, as it often became after Constantine, an end in itself.

Church attendance figures, whether increasing or declining, may be helpful to know. But the real question is not the quantity of members but the quality of members, not how many go to church at a special place on a special day but how many are the church every day in the world.

- - - - -

Although some of the following account of daily Bible reading at Central High School and its sequel is slightly exaggerated, or more than slightly, it's true that we did use the experience to learn as well as challenge one another's beliefs, a healthy practice. For the most part the names have been changed, naturally, to protect the guilty.

- - - - -

A Good Book for School
NVD February 17, 2003

Prayer in public schools continues to be an exciting debate about which I can't get at all excited. What I could get excited about is the introduction of daily Bible readings to the public schools.

I had an excellent experience from that practice in the 1950s at Philadelphia's Central High School, an all male, predominantly Jewish school.

One of our homeroom teachers, seriously underpaid, lightened his work load by having us students, in alphabetical order, select and read a passage of Scripture to begin each day while he sat at his desk and did paperwork.

Class lead-off, a Jewish lad, regularly used his opportunity to read something from the Hebrew Bible devastatingly derisive of gentiles. Next day I, out of the Christian tradition, would respond by reading a passage that would be grating to Jewish sensitivities: a claim about Jesus' divine sonship or resurrection; the Christian following me would continue the next day with another New Testament passage. But after him came a long string of Jewish students from whom we gentiles took a real biblical beating out of the Hebrew prophets.

Sometimes we Christians would get in some jabs by reading a passage from the Old Testament that was traditionally taken as a prophecy of Jesus, like the "virgin will conceive" in Isaiah; sometimes a Jewish student would track down and read something very pro Jewish from the New Testament, like John 4:22 where Jesus says, "Salvation is from the Jews".

Trying to find harassing passages for the class opening taught us all our way around the Bible, and then in the long and heated luncheon debates over the meaning of passages we came to understand and even respect one another's backgrounds and beliefs in ways we never would have if there hadn't been daily Bible readings. We learned to disagree intelligently and fight fairly.

Besides that, thanks to home-room Bible reading we learned long chunks of scripture by heart. You might think that probably wouldn't be very helpful to normal people, only to someone like me who turned out abnormal: a clergy person. In spite of the Hebrew prophets' invectives against Gentiles. But memorization proved helpful to a Jewish friend of mine and his whole neighborhood by healing a rift with reconciliation..

Our lead-off reader had once moved to neutral territory by reading a Psalm that said nothing derogatory against the gentiles, just sang the praises of the Creator, to which both communities could say amen. As a further gesture of good will, the next morning I read the same Psalm. The teacher said nothing and we all wondered how closely he was paying attention to this important opening exercise. So to test him the next in line read the same Psalm yet again. No comment from the teacher. The tradition continued on until we all had heard the Psalm so often we had it memorized.

"Time for a different passage, gentlemen," the teacher finally commented.

Next day in another amazing gesture of good will a Jewish lad read the thirteenth chapter of Paul's letter to the Corinthians. It was the New Testament, but had not a word about Jesus or the church or anything that a Jewish student would object to, just a description what kind of love is needed to hold a community together. We could all say amen to that too.

Again, by the time the teacher woke up to what was going on and stopped it, all of us had the passage memorized without even trying.

At one of our much later reunions Jerry Kaplan described how he had used that passage to astound his Christian next door neighbors and stop a major neighborhood argument.

He had built on his lawn the

traditional booth for the Jewish fall harvest festival of Succoth. Neighbors had come over to complain that the booth was an eyesore. Jerry pointed out that it would be up for only a week. Arguments about freedom of religion and freedom of expression grew heated.

In the midst of it he had quoted to the neighbors the whole chapter from Corinthians about being patient and kind and not insisting on your own way.

His gentile neighbors were so flabbergasted that he could quote the New Testament so extensively that they started asking him why he knew it and where he had learned it and did he believe it. Amid his responses and their subsequent discussion they forgot completely and forever about their resistance to the booth on his lawn. In fact they asked where in the Bible Succoth was described and learned a little about Deuteronomy 23: 39-43 and Jewish traditions.

I don't know if prayer is helpful in public schools. But I thus bear personal witness – something Lutherans rarely do – to a time when community concord was attained as a result of Bible reading in the public school!

- - - - -

I had previously enjoyed writing up two reflections on prayer. Remembering them and reflecting on the dynamics of my own prayer life I continued with yet another, as follows.

- - - - -

The Dynamics of Prayer
NVD February 24, 2003

Does God hear our prayers? Some people say yes, some say no. Many even say there is no such thing as a god – or goddess – to hear prayers. It unnerves me! Am I wasting my time when I pray?

I began to think about what all is or might be going on when I'm praying.

Certainly my image of what's going on when I pray

isn't literally accurate. When I pray I still have lurking in the back of my mind an image of an anthropomorphic figure somewhere up above cocking an ear to hear what I have to say. But I know that my image isn't what is really happening.

What really goes on in conversation? In human conversation when I talk to my wife I'm generating sound waves with my vocal cords and shaping them with my mouth. Air carries those waves until they hit her ear drums and set it vibrating. The vibrations are carried by nerves into her brain where neurons interact in such way that she can say she hears me. But she and I do all of that without any thought about the actual mechanics of the conversation process. The mechanics aren't "really" what's happening.

If there is a Creative Spirit with whom we can communicate, the mechanics of that communication are certainly not the same as those involving vibrating air and neurons. Perhaps prayer involves a nonphysical medium akin to extrasensory perception or mental telepathy about which we know or understand next to nothing. But as with my wife, so too with my Creator I can "talk" without thinking about the mechanics of the process. People were conversing, after all, long before they knew or understood how air vibrations and eardrums and neurons worked. People can pray without understanding how human thoughts can be "heard" (read? sensed? tuned in on?) by what is pure Mind.

But what if, as many claim, there is no such thing as a nonphysical being which can receive my messages, understand them, and respond to them? Am I wasting my time?

I decided I'm not. My prayer life helps me even if there is no Spirit out there to receive the messages I'm sending.

I'm sure people who don't believe a God exists take some time each day to count their blessings and thus develop a positive, grateful attitude towards life. But I find it much easier to count my blessings and be thankful if I picture a Source of blessings to which I'm responsible and can say "Thank you."

Even memorized prayers, as long as they're not simply rattled off by rote, can be helpful. The Lord's prayer's "Forgive us as we forgive others" reminds me not only that I need forgiveness but that I should give forgiveness. Any precomposed prayer can be a learning experience or reinforcement practice, probably with much more of an impact or effect on the psyche because of its dramatic conversational format than just the mental reminder, "I should be more forgiving."

Moreover, if prayer is only an imaginary conversation, it forces me to clarify my own thoughts and feelings. As in any good conversation, in prayer I need to be sensitive to the Person I'm addressing, whether that Person really exists and "listens" or not. I might be really angry with someone and want to say "Smash him in the teeth, Lord!" in company with Psalmist in 139 who asked God to smash his oppressors' babies on jagged rocks. Then I remember to whom – real or imaginary – I'm speaking. The prayer changes: Lord, I want him smashed in the teeth. But I know you don't want me reacting that way. Help me deal with and overcome my anger."

Conversation between God and me may thus be no more than an internal dialogue between my good self, projected as God, and my bad self. But it certainly is a useful exercise. Whether or not there is an objective Reality out there who hears and responds, imaginary conversations with an imaginary Being, pictured as good and one to whom I'm responsible and answerable is helpful.

Am I wasting my time in prayer? If there is no divine Person or if the Divinity isn't tuning in to me, in one sense I'm wasting my time. I'm not really involved in the kind of actual dialogue that I'm assuming I am. In another sense, however, I'm not wasting my time at all but engaging in a very creative and imaginative exercise that can be the equivalent of a deep conversation with the most excellent of therapists. Without having to pay a hefty fee.

- - - - -

As I was writing editorials I also was working on fiction: the mystery novel, *Testing the Spirits,* and a number of short stories with the same clergyperson sleuth. The following editorial was originally one of those short stories.

- - - - -

'So Help Me God'
NVD February 28, 2003

"So help me God" I got into real trouble when, wearing my clergy collar, I took the witness stand and was asked to swear that the testimony I was about to give was the truth, the whole truth, and nothing but the truth "so help you God."

"Which god?" I asked the bailiff administering the oath.

I figured it was a fair question. I didn't want to invoke the help of some strange god and have Mercury or Thoth or Quizlcoatl or my own suddenly breathing down my neck.

The bailiff shot a confused "What do I do now?" look at the judge, who at this point wasn't paying close attention. Well, not to the trial. To the musculature of a rather studly juror? Well, yes. Some judges don't pay close attention to the actual trial until later along. MUCH later along.

"There is only one god," the bailiff hesitatingly suggested.

"Not in my tradition," I responded. "Right there in the Ten Commandments, which I understand some judges post over their bench, it says 'You shall have no other gods before me.' That proves, at least in my tradition, that there are other gods. Which god's help am I asking for?'"

Hearing the words "some judges" had aroused the attention of this trial's judge, who did what some judges do so well: without having any real knowledge of what was going on they second guess what is happening and make a comment that turns out to be reasonably relevant. My original query "Which god?" she answered by saying "Your god."

I asked, "Is my God officially recognized by this court?"

Her eyes had "contempt of court" charges written all over them but she didn't say anything. I suspect she realized that she was in a serious bind. On the one hand if she claimed the court did recognize my god she was in all kinds of danger of violating the constitution's First Amendment by establishing religion. Headlines would blare "Judge Recognizes Lutheran God!" (Actually our god isn't really Lutheran, but you know how reporters work.)

On the other hand, if she claimed the court did not recognize my god she already guessed that I was enough of a wise-ass to ask "Then why does the court want me to swear by a god the court doesn't recognize?"

She was quick. She avoided any show of favoritism by responding, "This court recognizes all gods."

"And goddesses?" I asked.

Such a scowl I got. But the reporters' pens were poised and she had to say something. If she said "Goddesses too" the headlines would blare "Judge Acknowledges Existence of Goddesses" and she'd be in major trouble with a large segment of American society. If she said "Not goddesses" the headlines would blare, "Judge Denies Existence of Goddesses" and she'd be alienated from a small but exceedingly vocal segment of American society.

Off to chambers we went.

Out of earshot of reporters she accused me of clowning around with the judicial process and threatened to cite me for contempt.

I assured her that I was not clowning around, that I take the judicial process very seriously, and that not taking God's name in vain was a commandment I sincerely wanted to obey. So when the court wanted me to invoke God's help when I swear, I thought it was fair for me to know which god the court had in mind. It was, after all, their formula.

She screwed her face up, drummed her fingers on her desk, and, I'm sure, pictured how the headlines would read if she cited a clergyperson for contempt of court.

"Will you aver?" she finally asked.

"What's that?" I asked.

She explained that it was a formula for use by people who, out of religious commitment, will not swear in court. It would avoid "So help me God."

"Will that compromise my testimony?" I asked.

"No," she snapped back.

That made me feel better, so I agreed to aver instead of swear so help me God.

(The newspaper article ended at this point because of space constraints; the original submission continued with the following.)

We prepared to leave chambers. I wondered if the reporters would pick up on my averrance. If the headlines blared "Clergyman Denies God's Help!" what would my bishop say?

On the way out of chambers the judge sneezed.

"God bless you," I politely said.

"Oh, shut up," Her Honor | grumpily responded.

- - - - -

When the *Northern Virginia Daily* was preparing for its annual wedding insert I sent the following note with an article about a wedding, parts of which were actually true. The article was printed, but in a regular edition and not amid the lace and flowers supplement. Its original title, which I had enjoyed more than the one assigned by the paper, had been "Wedding Belle Blues."

John,
Unless you want it for contrast, the following is probably too much burlap and cactus for inclusion among the lace and flowers of your bridal insert, the date of whose publication I've forgotten. I do hope you have a clergy piece to balance all the "wedding as gaudy extravaganza" with "wedding as public profession of commitment." My own essay would probably fit better in a regular edition.
Enjoy!
        RKB

- - - - -

Candor an Unwelcome Wedding Guest
NVD March 1, 2003

Being honest, especially at wedding ceremonies, does not always pay among us clergy. My honesty at one wedding ceremony got me in such trouble with members of a former congregation that my bishop took steps to move me out of his jurisdiction.

Probably I had a bad attitude going into the ceremony. It was one of those weddings that all clergyfolk hate but are usually too charitable – or cowardly – to admit or to do anything about.

All the preliminary arrangements for scheduling the church, the organist, the sexton, and me were made by the bride's mother. Naturally I was always consulted last after the more important officials: DJ, limousine driver, caterer, hairdresser.

Moreover, in spite of my having mailed to the bride all the necessary information and having informed the mother repeatedly that I preferred to deal directly with the couple, the mother called regularly, not to the church office but to me at home at odd hours, to ask about such liturgically significant concerns as where they could place flowers and what angles they could take pictures from. And with each call she complained vehemently about the church's policy not to waste food by throwing rice. They had thrown rice at her wedding, she assured me.

I forbore to point out that back then the world's population was less in danger of starving because it was much smaller.

She also assured me, when I was even more abrupt on the phone than usual, that after all she and her husband were paying my salary.

That was true. Every Christmas eve and Easter morning they were there, and presumably put something in the offering plate. I could tell, however, that they didn't give a check or use an offering envelope because our financial secretary had no record of the extent of their generosity.

Yes, I was gauche enough to check.

Finally I had a chance to meet for several sessions with the happy couple. At least she kept insisting how happy they were. He was rather sullen and silent. We all put up with one another reasonably well. When she shot a warning glance at her groom and then lied to me that I was totally misinformed and they were definitely not living together, I let it pass. When I got in a cheap shot about her unfamiliarity with the layout of the church she claimed to love so dearly (she hadn't noticed we had started using a free standing altar six years previously) she let it pass.

During the rehearsal I yet once more remarked that since the couple was already living together it struck me as very artificial for the groom to come in from one direction and the bride from another. The bride and her mother insisted vociferously that the couple was not living together, the groom stayed silent and sullen, and all of the bridal party and groomsmen tittered.

So she rehearsed coming down the aisle on her father's arm and falling in next to the groom.

Her father stepped back.

"No, no," I directed him. "The tradition is that you stand between them to protect your daughter's virginity from this horny young rascal until they're ready to exchange vows so they can officially move in together."

No arguments. Guffaws from the groomsmen.

"Now I'll ask 'Does this relationship have your blessing?'" I told the bride's parent "We want you to say, 'Who giveth this woman?'" Momma told me, "We want her father to give her away."

My honesty finally overcame any desire to be kind.

"Face it, mom," I shot back loudly. "She gave herself away a long time ago. And very possibly not even to this guy."

From the family lots of silence, lots of sullenness. From the bridal party a few knowing smiles aimed at a groomsmen who had previously dated the bride and was turning crimson.

Next day the ceremony went beautifully. Parents gave no more arguments or suggestions. Bridal party and groomsmen were especially cheerful and cooperative. Bride and groom seemed totally anesthetized. I even behaved and forbore to step accidentally on the bride's train as the recessional began.

Trouble didn't start until a week later. Someone should have told me the bride's uncle was the used car salesman who always gave a good deal to my bishop.

- - - - -

My new involvement in the Shenandoah Astronomical Society rekindled my interest in astronomy and gave rise to another editorial on an astronomy theme. Carl Sagan can be heard in its opening line.

- - - - -

Lost in Space: Feel the Wonder
NVD March 8, 2003

Billions and billions of galaxies with billions and billions of stars over billions and billions of light years of space can be very intimidating. Some folk begin to feel lost and lonely, disoriented and diminished when they first learn of the vastness of our universe. Members of my congregations have often confessed to me feelings of helplessness or insignificance when they try to contemplate their place in the astronomically immense scheme of things.

When it comes to a feeling of belonging and being at home, however, or to a question of value and worth, what really counts? The quantitative counting up of tens to the twentieth power? Or the qualitative value that can be put on something apart from its size?

Western civilization since the time of the so-called enlightenment has often deceived itself with the misperception that bigger or more is automatically better than smaller or less. And as a corollary comes the erroneous deduction, often subconscious, that the universe, which is so huge, counts for virtually everything, and the human individual, so infinitesimal, counts for virtually nothing.

But value and worth are not necessarily based on size or numbers. Being massively overweight does not mean being healthy, and our school systems brag not about how large but about how small their class sizes are. Larger income sounds good, but a larger percentage for income tax does not. A cubic yard of coal is worth much less than a pea sized diamond, unless you need something to heat your house; but a pea sized diamond isn't worth a cubic yard of manure when you need something to fertilize your garden.

Sometimes bigger can be better; sometimes smaller can be better. It isn't size per se that determines value. And so there is no reason why the infinitesimal human individual can't be, as well as feel, worth as much as or even more than the almost infinite seeming universe.

Further complicating the feeling of personal discontent as very small creatures in a very large world, moreover, is our reluctance to accept limits. Built into us seems to be a desire for more and more – to acquire more, to do more, to go more places, to have more kinds of experience. In fact, maybe that innate desire is why we so easily mislead ourselves into believing more and bigger is better. And in the face of that desire it's a large frustration to encounter a universe that is too big to visit, explore, and experience first-hand. Perhaps too big for many of us even to picture or comprehend!

Acceptance of limitations is a sign of maturity. From playing the field, we choose, and limit ourselves to, one partner; among a broad variety of vocational possibilities we choose one as a career. We learn not to take those extra drinks late into the party, not to see how far we can push the car's speedometer. We learn to be content within limitations. So too as we look out over the beguiling, tempting, and intriguing vastness of space we can learn, in fact we have to learn, to be content not to be able even to name, let alone to visit and explore, the billions of stars in the billions of identified galaxies.

Trying to contemplate the size and complexity of the universe can provide a religious experience. Part of that experience includes feelings of awe and wonder arising from an encounter with mystery and majesty and accompanied by feelings of lostness and insignificance. Similar to the reactions many have to Carl Sagan or Jack Horkheimer graphically explaining the dimensions of the cosmos, I suspect it's the same mix of reactions that prompted Isaiah to say "Woe is me! I am lost" in his vision of an encounter with God (Isaiah 6: 5).

But with those emotional responses can come also two important ethical lessons: value does not necessarily depend on size, and as humans we face limitations which cannot but be respected.

- - - - -

My holiday pieces have had the best reception among editors and have been published most widely in a number of newspapers. This one also made its first appearance in the Wilkes-Barre *Times-Leader* in the mid-nineties, at the same time I was trying to straighten out Steve Corbett.

- - - - -

St. Patrick for Protestants
NVD March 15, 2003

St. Patrick's Day reminds me how poorly seminaries train us clergy for the real world.

St. Patrick wasn't Irish, as

most folk believe. In seminary we read his autobiography. He tells us himself that at the age of sixteen he was kidnapped from his family home in Britain and sold as a slave in Ireland. After six years he escaped, trekked across the Emerald Isle, and begged passage on a ship to return home. Later, a series of dreams convinced him God wanted him to travel again to the land of his captors as a missionary.

Try to tell them at a bar on St. Patrick's Day that the one who's become the patron saint of Ireland wasn't Irish. Seminary doesn't train us how to deal with that kind of conflict. (Seminary doesn't encourage us to hang out in bars, either; another of its inadequacies.)

St. Patrick didn't drive the snakes out of Ireland. The rumor or legend that Ireland had no snakes was already being circulated by the Roman poet Solinus a hundred years before Patrick, probably at the pay of an Irish Chamber of Commerce. As often happened, a later Christian leader received credit for something that had happened long before Christianity's arrival.

St. Patrick didn't use the shamrock to illustrate the Trinity. At the time of Patrick's fifth century mission to Ireland the doctrine of the Trinity was not yet clearly defined and would have been unknown to an untaught bumpkin way off in the British Isles who never went to – or even heard of – seminary. Patrick's autobiography makes no reference to the use of a shamrock. Actually, the first account of Patrick using a shamrock doesn't appear until the seventeenth century, more than a millennium after he died.

Seminary took me through the primary source materials and taught me the facts. The world believes the misinformation: Patrick was Irish; he drove snakes out of Ireland; he carried a shamrock. Seminary did not teach me an effective way of enlightening with the facts those folk who sit in the darkness of misinformation.

Never mind my credibility at the local bar: even in my authority position in the pulpit wearing my power robe my congregation didn't believe me about Patrick – and they're Lutheran. But they were more committed to the Patrick legend than Ss. Pius and Roman Down-the-Street. I quoted sources and even showed them the texts after the service. It made no difference. They believe what they want to believe.

I found a way the next year,

however, to distract them from the misinformation about Patrick, to give them a more important spin on Patrick so that they forget about the false image: Irish, snake-eliminating, shamrock-wielding. I point out that more important than his nationality was his commitment to sharing God's good news. The congregation, none of which is Irish, smiles agreeably.

I observe, quoting accepted environmental groups, that real snakes are our friends and more important was Patrick's willingness to drive out his own metaphorical snakes of anger and resentment towards the nation that had kidnapped him as a teenager and thus prevented him from attending a proper seminary. The congregation, who themselves wrestle regularly with snakes of anger and resentment and never attended a proper seminary, nods vigorously.

Building towards a crescendo, I shout "Forget the shamrock! Forget the Trinity! Remember that Patrick provides us an annual occasion for festivity and celebration!" The congregation audibly murmurs, "Amen."

Finally all my congregation believes me and leaps to its feet cheering when in a grand climax I announce the inevitable conclusion: St. Patrick must have been in fact a German Lutheran!

- - - - -

As a former professor of Classical Languages and Literature and a student of early Church history, I might be expected to have a special fondness for old time things. For some I do. But not for old time religion, as I explain in the following . . .

- - - - -

No 'Old Time Religion'
NVD April 14, 2003

"Gimme that ol' time religion" is a song I never sang with much gusto, partly because I'm unfamiliar with it since it doesn't appear in The Lutheran Book of Worship, but more than that because, in spite of the repetition of each line three times for slow learners like me, I just don't understand it.

What is it that makes "ol' time religion" more to be desired than "new time religion"?

I can't imagine people singing with verve, "Gimme that ol' time medicine." Who would want to go back to leaches and blood letting, snake oil and trepanning, to a time before antibiotics and anesthesia, hip replacements and open heart surgery?

I can't imagine people singing with enthusiasm, "Gimme those ol' time communications systems." Who would want to go back to times before telephones and television, e-mail and the internet, when it took five days for a letter to get to California and at least two weeks for a letter to cross the Atlantic by ship?

Ol' time lights – gas mantles instead of electricity? Ol' time heating – chopped and split wood instead of gas, oil, or electric? Ol' time home entertainment? Stereoptica and parlour games? Ol' time transportation – horse and buggy or Shanks mare instead of automobiles and airplanes? Ol' time food preservation and preparation? Ol' time vacation spots? Ol' time social and racial stratification?

There is, I admit, one area about which most folks might possibly sing with some spirit and with me joining in: "Gimme that ol' time politics". That's one facet of our society that seems to have worsened significantly rather than improved with the passage of time.

One of the real ironies is that congregations likely to sing lustily about "that ol' time religion" are also most likely to use the most newfangled electronic equipment: keyboards, mixers, and amplifiers, computer generated graphics and powerpoint projectors.

In contrast, many mainline denominations, which have kept up with modern discoveries and have dealt with the implications of the Dead Sea Scrolls and the latest in synoptic gospel research, psychological studies of their memberships and sociological studies of congregational dynamics, limit their media work to the ol' time flannelgraphs and organs.

One fundamentalist congregation with which I used to share monthly prayer breakfasts had put together a multimedia presentation for teenagers back in the early nineties. Four slide projectors ran sometimes in synch to produce a widescreen picture, sometimes each throwing a separate image. Sound came from a variety of speakers.

It was elaborate and sophisticated and indeed very modern. And towards the end of that high tech presentation they projected onto the screens, complete with a bouncing cross that followed the words, "Gimme that ol' time religion, Gimme that ol' time religion, Gimme that ol' time religion, It's good enough for me."

Ironic. The reason for the repetition of each line three times was so that members of ol' time congregations, before the creation of spirit duplicators or mimeographs, of photocopiers or overhead projectors, could pick up the words as they went along.

Religion itself is of course timeless, it's the trappings or methods of religion that change. The Power that created us can love and renew us whether our mental picture is of an old man sitting on a golden throne on the other side of a blue dome or a pure Spirit interwoven through the DNA within us and the galaxies at the ultimate red-shift limits of observation.

Problems arise when we try to hold onto the ol' time trappings of a golden throne on the other side of a blue dome after we've discovered the Creator did much more extensive and much more intricate creating than we had previously dreamed.

"It was good enough for Peter (repeat three times), it's good enough for me," runs the song. Alas, I must have strange tastes. I don't want a religion that's simply good enough. Especially simply good enough for a fisherman who never used an outboard motor or a sonar fish locator or a long distance radio weather report based on satellite surveys.

I don't want a religion good enough, I want a religion that's better yet, centered on the ol' time belief in God's existence and the specialness of God's people and Jesus and the cosmic change brought about by Good Friday and Easter, but a religion also able to incorporate into its belief and practice both the wide range of modern technologies and the sophisticated intricacies of modern understandings of humanity and the world.

- - - - -

"Why do other expression of the Christian faith believe the way they do?" I often ask myself when I find something in another denomination different from my church's expression of the Christian faith. At Princeton Seminary in the sixties I wrote a series called "Through Evangelical Eyes" for the student newsletter, *The Wineskin*, interpreting various Roman Catholic practices for the Protestant community. Since then in Bible studies I have led about life after death I've discovered among Protestants not only a willingness to hear the following rationale for purgatory but to accept it as a possibility. Don't tell their bishops!

- - - - -

Purgatory for Protestants
April 22, 2003

Lutheran clergy I may be, but I'm almost willing to accept the Roman Catholic belief in Purgatory, anathema though that traditionally is to Protestants. Don't tell my bishop!

Belief in Purgatory helped prompt Martin Luther's ninety-five theses, topics proposed for a debate that eventually split the western church. But at that stage of his thought Luther challenged not the existence of Purgatory but the misuse of Purgatory for fundraising: the sale of indulgences to hasten departed souls through the post mortem process.

Purgatory in Roman Catholic belief is a process of punishment and restitution, for past sins as a rehabilitation program for sinners, a preparation for entry into God's eternal feast. It happens in the between time after a person's death but before the end of the world at Christ's final return.

Of course there's no strong scriptural evidence for a Purgatory, only rare, obscure passages that might support belief in a time of waiting between death and resurrection like Jesus' words in John 5: 25-28. Paul, in 1 Corinthians 15:29, speaks of "being baptized for the dead", as if those who have died can in some way have their status changed by those still alive. Peter's first letter, 3:19, seems to describe Christ as preaching to those who have died. And 1 Corinthians 3:10-15 speaks about the last day's purifying fire. But all these passages are ambiguous.

Purgatory still makes sense

to me even though I don't like the idea. The process is painful and unpleasant.

"Purging", as with emetics and enemas, means to cleanse, to get rid of, and is not comfortable or pleasant. The process might even be viewed as a punishment, just as the dentist's drill or the surgeon's knife, both working for our health, are not comfortable but painful. Similarly, what goes on in the place of purging is the redisciplining of our wills, cutting out those surviving, deep seated reflexes of selfishness in order to have eternal wholeness. That process is painful whether it's done here or hereafter. The Purgatory theory is that what elements of my will and personality I do not reshape into saintly perfection here will be appropriately reshaped for me hereafter. It'll hurt.

In addition to purgatory as a state in which the soul is thus rehabilitated, it is considered the grace period after death in which people can pay penalties or accept punishment for misdeeds in this life. Even Luther in the fortieth of his ninety-five theses admits "A Christian who is truly contrite seeks and loves to pay penalties for his sins."

Although a sin is forgiven, the sinner naturally wants to do something to make up for the sin. If I willfully trample my neighbor's flowerbed and later sincerely apologize and am forgiven, I'll still want to make restitution and replace the flowers I damaged. Or, if I cannot replace something, I'll be willing to "serve time" helping my neighbor in compensation. Purgatory is "serving time" after death.

In the late medieval period right before Luther the time and punishment aspect began to outweigh the rehabilitation and restoration aspects. Further, it came to be believed that the penalty owed by one person could be offset or paid off by a good deed done by someone else. (My brother could replace my neighbor's trampled flowerbed for me.) Someone's gifts of charity, whether for helping the poor or rebuilding St. Peter in the Vatican's basilica, could cancel the punishment due for grandmom's greedy hoarding or grandpop's barroom brawls. The Papal office calculated what particular good deeds or charitable gifts cancelled how much punishment, tallied in numbers of years. It was this legalistic, bookkeeping approach that Luther attacked in his ninety-five theses.

Unfortunately I don't believe somebody else can do for me the rehabilitation work that needs to be done. I do believe that my personality will need to be very different in the new and perfect life to come. "Finish then thy new creation, pure and spotless let us be," as one of our Protestant hymns declares. And since I know I'm not going to achieve that purity and spotlessness fully in this life I'm willing to believe that all my remaining impurities and spots will be purged from me somewhere and sometime between my death and my sharing in eternal glory.

I also understand the desire to make restitution for wrongs I've done. Purgatory gives me the opportunity to do that task. In fact, it forces me to do it even when, as sometimes happens in this life, I'm a bit reluctant to say I'm sorry or straighten out problems I've caused, usually, of course, unintentionally and inadvertently.

If you do tell me bishop I'm willing to see some sense in the principles of Purgatory, be sure to tell him also that I don't like the idea, I'm forced into it simply by the logic of my faith.

- - - - -

The following two articles were behind the times if you consider them responses to the Scopes trial about teaching Darwin's theory of evolution in school, or else two years ahead of the times if you consider them input to the 2005 court hearing about Intelligent Design in the Dover School system in Pennsylvania. Among the predominantly academic tone of most of the public debate, the second editorial strikes, I think, a helpful note of personal witnessing: how I feel about the possibility of being a product of evolution and how my faith deals with the prospect. The topic is one worth monkeying around with, but I wouldn't want to go completely ape over it.

- - - - -

Religion, Revolution and Evolution
NVD May 5, 2003

Jesus' followers still argue among themselves and with others about the Theory of Evolution. Some are horrified by it;

others have no problem integrating it with their belief in a personal and caring Creator.

New scientific theories are often divisive.

Back in the early 1600's Copernicus' Theory of Revolution, that the Earth revolves around the Sun, had a disruptive impact on Jesus' followers similar to the impact of the Theory of Evolution today. At that time some were so horrified they excommunicated Galileo, himself a clergyperson who accepted Copernicus' theory; others integrated it into their view of the world without a major problem.

Today Copernicus' perspective has become pervasive: everyone, even among Christians, believes the earth revolves around the sun, rather than sits at rest in the center of the universe. As we wait for a similar acceptance of the Theory of Evolution as the way in which the Creator took earth, Adamah in Hebrew, and molded it into humanity, Adam, it might be helpful to review some dynamics of the Copernican Revolution.

Actually, any major shift of perspective is upsetting to most people, whether it involves a cosmic world-view or something personal like the discovery that a trusted public figure does not deserve public trust, or a forced vocational relocation to a strange area, or the revelation of an offspring's unexpected sexual orientation. We don't like unexpected changes.

Probably the anxiety after Copernicus' "revolution" was not so much about the shift of Earth from center to orbit as the fact itself of a shift: what had been long accepted was proven false. I suspect also that if it had been the other way around – if the Earth had long been assumed to be in orbit on the periphery but was discovered to be at rest at the center – the anxiety and upset and arguments and anathemas would have been just as strong.

But what real significance did the shift in perspective have? Does the layout of the universe tell us something about the nature of things and the role of humanity within it?

If earth were at the center, with sun, moon, other planets, and stars revolving around us, would that mean humans, earth's noisiest residents, were especially important? Does earth's location on the periphery mean that Earth, and we with it, are not really very significant in the total scheme of things?

It's true that the center sometimes does have a special importance: the center place at the table of honor, the center of the town or village where business was transacted, the gods and goddesses were worshipped, and court was held. We speak of "the center of attention".

But the center, after all, isn't necessarily important. Our eyes, which are not at the center of our bodies, are much more important to us than our belly buttons, which are at the center. If being at the center is really important, why hasn't the District of Columbia been relocated to the center of the United States?

Spatial location is not necessarily a sign of importance. If humanity has a special significance, we have it whether we live at the center or on the fringe; if Albert Einstein had a special significance to our understanding of space and time, he had it whether he lived in a major population center or a small town that's really a satellite of Trenton, New Jersey.

All of us as individuals think that we are important. Each of us is, in a non-spatial sense, the center of our world. Naturally all of us as a species project that. We assume we are important and special in the total scheme of things. (Perhaps we in fact are!) At one era in our human history our belief that humanity dwelled at the physical center of all things supported our impression that we were special and important.

Discovering that we were not at the physical center of things did not necessarily mean that we are insignificant or unimportant. In fact, a case could be made that since Copernicus humanity has come to consider itself more important and significant than it had before Copernicus: humanity has become more self-centered since it has lost the center place. Maybe it's a kind of cosmic psychological compensation.

In the course of centuries Jesus' followers adjusted to and accepted Copernicus' revolutionary theory. Some of Jesus' followers have similarly adjusted to and accepted evolution without losing faith in a God who creates, guides, and holds us accountable. Others of Jesus' followers are not there yet. And it will probably be a longer process this time because we're dealing not with how the world is laid out but how we ourselves came to be here. But eventually the view which some people today consider revolting will be accepted. Copernicus' revolution has shown us that even Christians can evolve.

Up from the Slime
NVD May 20, 2003

Humanity's origin either as a molding of clay by the hands of God or as a significant change in the DNA within the ape family over a long time period is hotly debated. Unfortunately the heat is generated because the question is reduced to a simplistic "either the Bible or evolution."

As a clergy person I prefer to use a "both - and" approach.

Of course I believe God had a hand in humanity's creation. I'm not sure, however, that each hand had four fingers and a thumb as ours do. Six fingers and two thumbs for more flexibility in the extensive task of creating the whole universe? Or are just one divine finger and one divine thumb enough? And how large are the fingers that could both place in orbit stars thousands of times larger than Earth and yet also mold the snowflake? God's "hand" must shrink or enlarge with the medium being manipulated. Or is God's "hand" just a metaphor for the creative activity of a spiritual Power who has no physical attributes or appendages?

Scripture often uses anthropomorphic imagery, but it would be a shame to get so caught up in it as to lose sight of its meaning: to ask, for example, if God's laugh (Psalm 2:4; 37:13; 59:8) is a guffaw or belly laugh, with or without slapping of the knee, or if God's ride upon the clouds (Isaiah 19:1; Psalm 68:4) is straddling or sidesaddle.

Use of human imagery to describe divine activity is indeed gripping and graphic. Read Exodus 33:21-23! But certainly this kind of imagery is no more to be taken literally than is Jesus' commandment, "If your right hand causes you to sin, cut it off!" (Matthew 5:30)

I believe, as Luther's catechism expresses it, "that God has created me and all that exists . . ." I do not believe, however, that my creation was by Divine Hands gently inserting a mini-me into my mother's uterus. I was created, I started life, when a very tiny sphere of protoplasm, drifting slowly down a warm tunnel of tissue, encountered an even smaller tadpole-like piece of protoplasm that had been furiously whipping its tail to win an upstream race against fifty million others.

Believing that's how I was created by God as an individual, I have no problem believing that God created the whole human race through modifications in the DNA of some hairy primates.

Scripture's first account of humanity's creation simply says, "So God created Adam/Man/humanity in God's own image, male and female God created them." Without reference to molding clay, this comes at the end of a chapter in which everything is created by God's Word; "God said let there be . . . and there was. . ." The second chapter account – refining or supplementing the first story? – describes God creating not by mere command but in much more human terms: first molding Adam/Man/humanity of earth (Adamah in Hebrew) and then, after planting a garden and forming animals and leading them to the man, creating not from earth but from a rib "The Woman", later named "Eve", Genesis 3:20.

Both stories, or the variations of one story, agree that God created humanity and gave us a special place in creation and holds us answerable. I agree. But between the two units of narrative the method and time sequences of humanity's creation are certainly different. That doesn't prevent agreement with the stories' basic meanings.

The Bible's description and the evolutionist's description need not be pitted against one another. The real dividing question is "Do you believe a Spiritual Power is responsible for the creation of humanity and holds humanity in general and individuals in particular responsible for their actions, OR do you believe that humanity arose by accident and is not responsible?" Both those who believe in the whole Bible literally and those of us who see some parts of the Bible as metaphor can join in saying yes to the first part of the question and then work together.

Unfortunately the creation debate too often centers not on what the Bible means, but on how the Bible expresses its meaning: always literally? Or sometimes literally and sometimes figuratively.

Liberal Christians and fundamentalist Christians should both be able to agree that God can work in, with, and under natural processes and go on from there. As it is, however, fundamentalists tend to lump liberal Christians in with atheists, and atheists, making no distinction between liberal and fundamentalist Christians, dismiss us all as unscientific conservatives.

More important than the question of how God created humanity is the question of how in spite of all our differences can atheist and Christian, liberal and fundamentalists, Jew and Muslim, work together for justice, peace, and well being.

- - - - -

I've always had this problem in congregations: what I say flippantly they take seriously and what I say in all seriousness they laugh off as a joke. It happened with the following editorial as well. Someone took seriously my tongue-in-cheek suggestion and responded that he did not think it would be possible "within the current boundaries of American jurisprudence." I hadn't really thought so either.

- - - - -

Churches Should Sue
June 19, 2003

Bringing lawsuits has become a national pastime. Groups and people sue at the drop of a hat – or the spill of hot coffee – as part of that great American drive to get rich quick. Probably churches shouldn't play that game. Not a lot, at least. But maybe we could get in on at least some of the action.

After all, religious communities have regularly borrowed customs and practices from surrounding cultures. Yiddish, for example, is a borrowing and adaptation of the German language by Jewish people in German speaking countries. Or consider the way in which the first night of Passover differs from all other nights because diners recline instead of sitting upright: a Jewish borrowing and adaptation of pagan Roman banqueting practice.

Through the centuries the church has borrowed from the surrounding culture of pagan Rome such things as genuflection and prayer rhetoric, from the Druids the hanging of mistletoe and the decoration of sacred evergreen trees, and even from the Germanic spring fertility goddess the term "Easter".

Today, however, Christians borrow too little from American culture. Groundbreaking for a new church or synagogue starts off with rabbi, priest, pastor, or board chairman turning over a clump of earth with the same cultural implement used in ancient civilization as far back as Abraham: the shovel. Next day modern civilization's technology comes in and the antiquated shovel is replaced by the serious modern tools of back hoe and bulldozer.

Synagogues and churches have put some of modern technology to religious use, like replacing the synagogue's jahrzeit candles or the church's votive candles with electric lights. But no significant use has been made of high tech, fun stuff like lasers or strobes. Rock concerts unfortunately make more dramatic impact in our society than our worship services.

More useful, however, than the church's borrowing the use of bulldozers, lasers, or strobes would be its taking advantage of that one special feature of early twenty-first century American culture.

The Church needs to get into law suits.

Christmas is a good place to start. "Christmas" is, after all, a Christian monopoly. But the word is plagiarized and used in all kinds of inappropriate settings. So for the first step let the churches bring suits against all those who misuse the term "Christmas" in ways that corrupt its meaning: for example, sue any office or business that has an annual "Christmas" party where drunkenness and lechery are more noticeable than a celebration of Jesus' birth.

Second, after having won enough damage judgments for all the misuses of "Christmas", establish a copyright royalty fee for its use in ways that do not run completely counter to its real meaning. Think of the income churches would derive from royalties on the term "Christmas candy"!

In addition to defending its rights to the term "Christmas" the Church can follow the same procedure with "Easter". Let New York city pay a hefty fee for sponsoring an "Easter" parade and let there be a special tax on any chapeau that's advertised as an "Easter" bonnet. And imagine the royalties that can be received simply from songs that use the term "Easter".

Eventually, use by non-Christians of practices like crossing the fingers or knocking on wood, and use of terms like "gospel truth" or "Good Samaritan" could also become grounds first for lawsuits and later for royalties.

When I suggested these ideas to a rabbi friend of mine he reminded me that without its Jewish antecedents Christians would have no "Christmas". "Christ", he reminded me, was only a Greek word translating the Hebrew word "meshiach", or "messiah", meaning "anointed". The concept of Christ or Messiah is plainly and unquestionably Jewish. I had to agree with him.

Hey, I believe in being fair. Take all the income churches derive from lawsuits against people or institutions which have misused "Christmas" and all the income from groups paying royalty on "Christmas" and split it fifty-fifty with Jewish communities as a gesture of ecumenical solidarity.

And cross your fingers (if you're a Christian or are willing to pay the "Christian practices fee") that our Jewish brothers and sisters bring no law suits against the churches for everything else that we've borrowed from them, from the word "Amen" down to the adapted form of Jewish seder we do with bread and wine every Sunday. After all, that would be carrying the levying of lawsuits way too far. (Interested lawyers, please respond to: bohmhome@shentel.net)

- - - - -

Not all of the following five essays about Noah's ark were published in the *Northern Virginia Daily*. Two made it through the presses, but then I accepted an interim pastoral assignment in Riegelsville, Pennsylvania, in spring of 2003 and the last three did not come out at that time. The third was finally published September 8, 2006. The fourth and fifth are still in the "awaiting publication" file at the *Northern Virginia Daily*.

Parts of these essays have popped up in various sermons and Bible studies I have done over the last twenty years, spin-offs of a solo clown presentation I had first written for a small church in Pennsylvania's Pocono mountain area. We invited the local synagogue folk to join us and share sailing on "Ark Earth" for an hour. My clown script is available, with other clown sketches, at my website, www.AltarEgoPub.com.

Later, while serving St. Paul, Dallas, Penna., I adapted the original performance for their remarkable clown troupe, fifteen people ranging in age from early teens to mid-seventies. They presented an excellent production to a standing room only crowd.

Further along, in 2003 when I was invited back to St. Luke, Shoemakersville, for an anniversary celebration, the lessons for the day included part of the flood story and the comparison of baptism to Noah's flood in 1 Peter 4. In addition to preaching about Noah's ark that Sunday I distilled from my previous Noah's ark material five editorial reflections as a special anniversary gift to the congregation.

Finally, I incorporated some of the material in an outdoor summer service on the lawn of St. Mark Church, Mechanicsburg, Pennsylvania.

My challenge in the one essay for someone to calculate how much water it would take to cover the earth to Mount Everest's height was actually taken on by a member of the adult class at Zion Stone Church, New Ringgold, when I was leading a Bible study. Alas, I forget the results, which were expressed by ten to the something power cubic units of water.

Interestingly, both Zion Stone Church and St. Luke, for whom the five essays were written, were combined Lutheran and United Church of Christ congregations which I had helped amalgamate. Thus as congregations of two separate denominations sharing one pastor and one building they were embodiments of the Noah's ark experience of creatures sharing the same space.

- - - - -

Earth is Our Ark
NVD June 23, 2003

Noah's ark is very popular. Card stores and gift shops have whole display areas with banners and figurines, pictures and models, plaques and posters of Noah's ark. It is also one of the most popular Biblical themes for cartoons.

Lighthearted treatment of the ark story as a fun thing is strange because the story itself has a very tragic dimension: the destruction of all but a few living things on earth because of humanity's misbehavior. Lurking therefore behind the happy scene of aardvarks and antelopes, mice and kangaroos, all smiling blissfully over the deck rails, is a grim picture of elephants and giraffes, rabbits and deer swimming bravely through the rising waters until they weaken, struggle frantically to keep their heads above water, and finally succumb to drowning.

For all this tragic background to the story, it is usually pictured and treated at least positively, if not comically. Those fortunate beasts peering from the deck show no grief or remorse that their parents and children, siblings and cousins, have breathed the fatal waters of the flood. The Noah story is not treated as a tragedy of destruction and death but as the celebration of a triumph of survival. Emphasis is not on the many who died, but on the few who survived. The story does not dwell on danger and loss but presents the message that in the midst of devastation and death, grimness and grief, there can nonetheless be hope and even deliverance.

One reason for the popularity of the Noah's ark story is its nonsectarianism. It's not about the Jewish people, although it appears in the Hebrew Bible. It's not about Christians or Muslims, although it is also part of their scriptures. The Noah story is appealing because it is about all humanity. It gives reassurance that God cares not just for the sons and daughters of Abraham and Sarah, not just for those who have been baptized, not just for those with allegiance to Allah, but for all living things, and it further bears witness out of one particular faith tradition that the Creator of all things is interested not just in people of one particular religion, race, or national origin, but loves all and has made a pledge and promise to the whole world never again to initiate mass destruction.

Yet a second reason for the popularity of the Noah's ark story is the way in which this ancient story dramatically represents our modern view of the human situation as we've come to experience it. The earth on which we live seems much smaller now and also more diverse than it did centuries ago. Five hundred years ago and more, in the face of dissension or opposition it was possible to pull up stakes and move to the provinces or sail to a new world or load the wagons and head west. Today we have instead a sense of all being trapped together on a small planet, like the animals all confined together on Noah's ark.

Like popular pictures of Noah's ark with its wild mix of skunks and squirrels, of lions and tigers and bears, we're all stuck on this planet with one another in all our bewildering variety – Democrats and Republicans, straights and gays, Roman Catholics and Baptists, male and female, Christians and Muslims, black and white, young and old, management and labor, Yale and Harvard, Iraqi and American.

Ark earth floats through the cold and fatal darkness of space, bearing a wonderful menagerie of very different but interdependent human beings and animals who need to work at getting along with one another for the duration in spite of their differences. The ark story is popular because it's so much more than a quaint story about Noah's family and the animals caught in a flood millennia ago. The story strikes a sympathetic chord in our psyches because it's a story about us: Earth is our ark and we're on it together.

Noah's Ark: Truth and Fiction
NVD July 3, 2003

"Pastor, Pastor, they've discovered Noah's ark!" folks excitedly tell me after having seen a television show or read a magazine article or a check-out line newspaper that regularly reports the discovery of Noah's ark.

"How big was it?" I always ask.

"Couple hundred cubics," usually comes the answer. "Like it says in the Bible."

"Four hundred fifty by seventy-five cubits," I correct them. "Did they say how a few hundred different species of animals managed to fit into an area smaller than a football field? Together with enough food to keep them alive for forty days?"

"Must have been a miracle," they sigh.

There must have been other miracles as well.

Back when the Noah story circulated in oral traditions before it was written down the general view of the world was that the sky was really a transparent dome – the "firmament" holding up "the waters above the firmament" (Genesis 1:6-7). It made sense. It was as blue up there as the Mediterranean. And rain was obviously from leaks in the firmament. And there was more than enough water up there to cover the earth, whose true dimensions and shape hadn't yet been calculated.

Today our different view of the world raises the question: where did all that water come from? It must have been a miracle!

Calculate how much water would be needed to cover the entire planet Earth from Dead Sea level, the lowest point on the surface, to the highest point, the tip of Mount Everest. That total volume of water is more than that available on the planet, even if the ice caps melted.

Where did all that extra water come from without a miracle?

Yet another miracle is needed. Calculate the weight of that extra volume of water. Then calculate how much the extra weight would distort the earth's orbit around the sun. God must have been busy not only with the miracle of producing all that extra water but also with the miracle of keeping the earth in orbit in spite of a massive weight change.

Sometimes I raise the need for these extra miracles with the person excited about the discovery of Noah's ark.

"Well, God can work miracles," they reassure me.

"But why?" I respond. "Why not simply wipe out humanity by divine command? A simple snuff by a single snap of the divine fingers? Why all the extra bother?"

"Who are we to question God?" they conclude.

I usually forebear to point out that God, like any good parent or teacher, invites and welcomes our questions. And when the story doesn't fit the facts it's time to reconsider.

Stories can make important points without being literally true. The Israelites didn't respond to Jotham's story (Judges 9:7-10) by saying, "But trees can't talk!" Jesus' stories about the prodigal son or the good Samaritan make their points even if they are only parables and not records of actual events.

So too with the story of Noah's ark.

Perhaps there was an actual worldwide flood that gave rise to the Noah story. Or maybe there actually was some structure – ark or raft or whatever – that once saved a local family and some of their livestock during a local flood. And the story was retold and grew in the retelling until it reached the worldwide proportions in which it's recorded in the Bible.

"It was as if the whole world were under water," we can imagine flood victims saying even today. And in ancient oral tradition such a remark could have easily grown into quite a story.

More important than whether or not the story of Noah's ark is literally true in every detail, or an embellished and exaggerated version of a local flood story, or pure fiction, God encouraged its retelling in oral traditions and its eventual recording to make the point: although there are times when human violence may bring on massive destruction, the Creator has at heart the best interests of beasts and human beings and has pledged and promised to work with and through them to maintain peace and harmony as they and we float on through space on ark-earth.

Noah's Ark: A Two by Two Story
September 8, 2006

How did the animals come on the ark? Two by two, or, as the popular Sunday School song has it, "The animals, they came on, they came on by Twosies, twosies." Says so right in Genesis 6:19: "You shall bring two of every kind into the ark."

But wait. Genesis 7:2 clearly says "Take with you seven pairs of all clean animals and a pair of the animals that are not clean."

Two by two or seven pairs? And if you can't trust the Bible, what can you trust?

Consider further. Genesis 8:20 reports that Noah sacrificed two each of the "clean" (kosher) beasts. But if there were only two of every animal, what remained after Noah and his family sacrificed the "clean" beasts? The only beasts left to be fruitful and multiply would have been the "unclean beasts." Keeping kosher would have become impossible; only the pigs and other trafe animals would have survived to provide dinners for future generations.

Come to think of it, how

did Moses know which beasts were "clean" and "unclean". That divine revelation didn't occur until after Moses led the Hebrew people out of Egypt (Leviticus 11; Deuteronomy 14).

Noah's wonderful story seems actually to have existed in two different versions, probably oral traditions, which were woven together later into the form in which they were written down in Genesis 6 - 9. That there were two views, two "takes" on the same story is a lesson in itself.

One of the two traditions reported two of every animal and ended with the rainbow, the other tradition reported seven pairs and ended with sacrifice.

Compare Genesis 6:5-8 with Genesis 6:11-22. Each is an introduction to the story of Noah's ark and each repeats the material of the other. But the first uses the term "LORD", all capitals, to replace the Hebrew letters of the divine name, y, h, w, h. (After all, the safest way to obey the commandment not to take the divine name in vain is not to say or write it at all except in sacred Torah texts.) The second passage, the other tradition, uses the generic term God, translating the Hebrew title "Ellohim."

How does the story of Noah's ark end? Everyone is familiar with the rainbow. But actually that's the ending in the "God" and two animal tradition. The alternate ending in the LORD and seven animal tradition reports that Noah sacrificed and roasted kosher animals, as would happen much later in the Jerusalem temple.

One version of the flood story, then, is very strong in its Jewishness: it uses the special, divine name of God revealed to Moses in Exodus 3:15, makes a distinction between unclean and clean, kosher, animals, and concludes with sacrifice. Apparently the oral tradition through which this version of the flood story passed had added later features, in the same way in which an oral tradition about the American revolution might anachronistically work in references to the United States or the Bill of Rights, neither of which came into existence until after the war.

The other version uses "God", a more general term than the proper name, treats all animals the same, and concludes with a rainbow and a covenant with all humanity.

Tightly interwoven but with obvious differences, these two stories provide a variation on the important lesson that with all our differences we're on ark-earth together and we need to cooperate. Two variant accounts of one event remind us that we do not always see things the same way or emphasize the same things. But rather than argue about minor differences – was it two of every animal or seven pairs? – we can more profitably agree on a major point – the Creator is lovingly concerned about all living things getting along with one another. And so too should we.

Noah's Ark: Beyond Religion
Unpublished

Noah's story in the Bible is set in a time before God began showing special interest and favor towards one particular, chosen people, the Jews. It's not until three chapters after the flood that God calls Abram and Sara and promises them offspring that will be "my special people" with Christians and Muslims joining in later along.

Noah, then, is a story from the Jewish heritage but not exclusively for the Jewish people, or for the Christian or Muslim communities that grew out of them. It's a story about all humanity and for all humanity, set in a time before the story about the division of humanity into different languages after the Tower of Babel (Genesis 11). And it says something important about relationships among different religions or even the non-religious.

Biblical scholars have unravelled from the written text of the Noah story two slightly different versions, presumably out of two different oral traditions before the Bible recorded them. One version was strongly Jewish: the use of the special Name God revealed to Moses, the distinction between kosher and unclean animals, and the offering of sacrificial animals; the other had a more universalist appeal.

Both traditions include, however, a divine promise. The one, with a more anthropomorphic picture of the Deity, reports that "the LORD smelled the pleasing odor" of the sacrifices and, apparently in a good mood after breaking a forty day abstention from burnt offerings, makes the promise "in his heart", though not out-loud to Noah, that never again would the earth be cursed and left unproductive because of human sinfulness (Genesis 8:20-22).

The other version concludes with the rainbow story, the more popular tradition, often displayed in depictions of Noah's ark. The greater popularity of the rainbow rather than the burnt offering is easily explained. Both in the days of oral tradition before the Bible was written and also now, everyone can see a rainbow. Not everyone did or does offer sacrifice from animals considered clean, "kosher".

Within the rainbow tradition is the recommissioning of all humanity: "Be fruitful and multiply", the same command given in the creation story. The repetition is like a sign that humanity is getting a new beginning, a resurrection. Moreover, God speaks a strong injunction against the violence which was God's reason for causing the flood in the first place. God expresses expectations that all the offspring of Noah and his wife, all humanity, will work at getting along with one another.

Humanity has not followed through. Rival claims of differing religious communities, as well as political communities or ethnic communities, often lead to the kind of hostility, strife, and warfare that provides ammunition for letters to the editor blaming religion for all humanity's problems. But the Noah story, although out of the Jewish, Christian, and Islamic tradition, claims that God's original expectation was that all people that on earth do dwell should get along with one another.

God's covenant with Noah's family prompted rabbis to make a distinction between this "Noachine covenant" with all humanity and the specialized "Abramic covenant" with just the Jewish people. Contemplating the Ten Commandments, rabbis testified that God does not expect all humanity to keep the "first table" of the divine law: having no God other than the One who led Israel out of Egypt, keeping that divine Name sacred, and observing the Sabbath. But God does, the rabbis agreed, expect all humanity to keep the "second table" of the divine law, refraining from violence and adultery, robbery and fraud.

In the rabbis' view, then, the offspring of Noah's family need not first become Jewish or, by extension, Christian or Muslim, to be responsible to the Creator of all for working against the use of force and violence and for justice and cooperation.

On ark-earth it's all right to be different, as long as you refrain from violence and work towards harmony!

Noah's Ark: Don't Rock the Boat
Unpublished

People's enjoyment of animals helps make Noah's ark so popular. If people did not enjoy animals, then people would not keep pets; zoos, those limited replicas of Noah's ark, would not be able to stay open; children's beds would not look like miniature Noah's arks with their scattered arrays of stuffed bears and kittens, lions and dolphins, snakes and toucans; and there would be no appeal in stories where toads, rats, moles, piglets, owls, rabbits, foxes, or rabbits all talk.

Noah's ark does more, however, than just appeal to our enjoyment of animals. It presents a picture of humanity as responsible for animals, of needing to take care of them.

Noah's family had to provide room and food for the animals on their ark and take care of them for forty days and nights. How often did the humans have to intervene when a leopard with a hungry look inched closer to a llama, or have to put a splint on the leg of a gangly giraffe who had sprained it by slipping on the poopy deck?

As the humans on the ark needed to care for the animals, so too humans in the twenty first century have begun to realize our responsibility and to take more seriously our need to care for the walruses and whales, the rats and rhinos, the beavers and badgers with whom we sail along on ark-earth.

Scriptural support for ecological sensitivity is weak in the twenty-seven Christian books of the Bible. Writers of that section expected the end of this world within their lifetimes so there was no need for precepts for care of the planet. But since the world didn't end in the first, second, or even sixteenth century, we need to look behind the "New Testament" for directions about caring for the planet.

Ecological sensitivity, though not strong in the Hebrew Bible, is nonetheless there. The same part of the Book that brought us the story of Noah's family has given us some guidelines for taking care of the birds and beasts with which we share this planet.

Deuteronomy 22:6-7 was the first passage to catch my attention as an ecological guideline or mandate. I was exploring the 603 commandments, by rabbinic count, beyond the basic ten and found: "If you come on a bird's nest . . . with the mother sitting on the fledglings or eggs, . . . let the mother go, taking only the young for yourself."

In our treatment of our fellow beasts that verse strikes a significant balance between killing anything at any time indiscriminately on the one hand and total abstention from any killing at all on the other. The mother bird, already grown and able to reproduce, is allowed to go free, presumably to be able to reproduce again. The eggs and the fledglings, whose chances for survival are much lower than their mother's, dare be eaten. (How hungry would you have to be to bother with most bird eggs or fledglings? Some divine irony lurks in this commandment.)

Maintaining a balance in nature, which seems to be the thrust of this commandment, is in fact a continuing theme in the Hebrew Bible. Read Psalm 104's description of God's establishment of balanced boundaries: grass for cattle, wine and bread for humans, nighttime for animals to prowl, daylight for humans to work; mountains for goats, rocks for coneys.

Balanced opposites as basic to the natural order are a recurring theme in Genesis 1: evening and morning, light and darkness, dry land and water, waters above the dome and waters under the dome, male and female.

Modern science also sees balance as a basic natural principle, from the balance of centrifugal and centripetal forces that keep the planets in orbit to the balance of positive and negative particles at the subatomic level.

Maintaining balance seems to be a good scriptural principle for working with nature. And maintaining balance is obviously a good principle for keeping a ship afloat, whether it's a small rowboat, Noah's ark, or ark-earth.

- - - - -

During my time at St. Peter, Riegelsville, Pennsylvania, 2003-2004, I did much writing but saw only one editorial published. I thought Mel

Gibson's movie "The Passion of the Christ" deserved some comment and the *Intelligencer* out of Doylestown in Bucks County had the intelligence to publish it.

The editorial, written before the movie was actually released, included guesswork about the flogging scene and strong reliance on John's Gospel. The guesses proved to be accurate.

- - - - -

Gibson Film Promises Impact Different from the Bible
February 23, 2004

Imagine how a Hollywood director, Mel Gibson for example, would present in a movie what appeared in a novel simply as, "Then they went to bed together and made love." What is brief in the written medium would have to be much fuller in the visual medium, with unavoidable shots of thrashing limbs and heaving sheets or naked bodies, and on the accompanying soundtrack appropriate noises, or inappropriate depending on your cinematic taste.

So, too, with Mel Gibson's visual presentation of the written text of the crucifixion of Jesus. Where the Bible passages say simply, "After flogging Jesus" (Mark 15:15, with parallels in Matthew 27:26 and John 19:1), the movies will perforce present the repeated lash of the whistling whip punctuated by sharp cracks and bloody slashes opening Jesus' back as he writhes beneath each blow. Obviously the description can be done in written form, though the Gospel writers chose not to do so.

The bottom line is that Mel Gibson's "The Passion of the Christ" will make a qualitatively different impact from the reserved tone of the Bible's written text.

One reason for the difference is the simple fact that visual presentations automatically differ from written ones. Another reason is a difference in intent. Mel Gibson follows a fundamentalist agenda of wanting to present to the audience exactly what happened, on the assumption that the Bible is a totally infallible historical source.

The Gospel writers themselves, however, were not primarily interested in writing a strict and accurate historical account of exactly what happened. Their purpose was to interpret a rather lose account of what happened in two ways.

First, they wanted to link Jesus' crucifixion with Hebrew Bible antecedents by quoting again and again, "As it was written . . ." or "This was to fulfill the passage . . ." These written commentaries, one of the Gospel writers' most important interests, would be difficult to work into a movie unless they were put on the lips of bystanders, which would not be true to what the Bible actually says.

Second, Gospel writers needed not to explain in detail what crucifixion was like. It was common enough that everyone at the time knew what it was like. But they needed to justify to strangers how someone considered by a minority to be God's own son managed to wind up being executed by the authorities as a common criminal.

Further complicating a film about Jesus' crucifixion is the fact that each Gospel writer presents a slightly different story or picture of Jesus. The first three Gospels set the crucifixion on the first day of Passover; John sets it on the day before Passover. The first three do not think it important to report Mary's presence by the cross; John is the only one to mention it. Will Gibson's version follow the three quarters majority and omit Mary, or fall in with the one quarter minority and include her?

Compare the anguished human figure of Jesus sweating blood in Luke 22:40-44 and pleading not to have to go through with what awaits him with the regal, majestic figure of Jesus before whose words even hardened Roman soldiers fall helpless to the ground in John 18:3-11. Which will Gibson follow or include?

My own bet is that whenever there's a choice, Gibson will follow John, the least historically reliable of the Gospels according to a majority of biblical scholars who are not fundamentalist.

As more and more intelligent Americans know less and less about what the Bible actually says, Gibson's film will serve the purpose of using the modern taste for shock, horror, and gore to lure them in to experience a presentation of Jesus' crucifixion in ways the Gospel writers hadn't intended.

That's a good start, I guess. But I would hope also that he intends to do a sequel on the part of the total story most emphasized by early believers but lacking in shock, horror, and gore: God's raising Jesus from the dead.

- - - - -

My first series of editorials was never published in a newspaper but circulated among a Lenten Wednesday Bible study I was doing at St. Paul Lutheran Church, Shavertown, Pennsylvania in 1996. In preparation for our Easter celebration of Jesus' resurrection I was reviewing with the group Biblical texts about what happens after death. Most people have the picture in their heads, from Greek philosophical thought, of souls leaving the body at death and going off to "heaven." Actually the only biblical characters who go off to heaven are Elijah, in a chariot, and Jesus, under his own steam (Acts 1:9), both with their bodies, not as ghosts. Traditions claim also that the bodies of Enoch (Hebrews 11:5) and Moses (Jude 9) were taken off to heaven. And although there's no Biblical account of it, there's an old tradition, honored in the Roman Catholic and Orthodox communions, that Mary was assumed bodily into heaven. Most Protestants tend to think that's assuming too much. In the Biblical view, everyone other than those five wait around in the grave until they are awakened and raised up. Check what Paul says, for example, at 1 Thessalonians 4: 15-17 or Martha, speaking to Jesus at John 11: 23-24.

Our Bible study was going to focus on the scriptural texts; I wanted to put in the group's hands ahead of time some kind of overview because dealing with those texts often upsets people by altering their deeply held convictions. So I wrote the first essay, expressing skepticism about "immortal souls." I wove in for the first time the theme "Don't tell my bishop." I had no serious reason at the time for doing so; I was just having fun. But looking back I suspect it was a veiled admission that what I was claiming, though well known and accepted by any bishop, would seem strange and even heretical to most church goers. Asking them to share with me in keeping a secret from the bishop, not always a popular figure in Lutheran congregations, might put them on my side.

One group member weeks later told me he thought my comments about the bishop indicated that I had serious problems with authority figures; most in the group knew my style well enough not to take those comments seriously.

I wondered how the group would respond to the first essay and I imagined two schools of response: firm Bible believers and New Age folk. As if the first essay had been a published editorial to which people had responded, I wrote two more essays. By that point I was hooked on the editorial style format and continued with it.

As I wrote, the more I wrestled with the concept of resurrection rather than immortality of the soul, the less I liked it, though I was forced to it both by the Biblical witness and biological science. So I wrote "Retraction," which we never had a chance to discuss in the class. By that point some in the group were sharing stories about contacts they thought they had had from deceased relatives and discussing how to draw the line between wishful thinking and fact. "Retraction" claims the only thing to survive death is the ability to make choices. Memory goes when our gray matter goes. I don't like to accept that, but I console myself, not very convincingly, with an extension of Augustine's analogy.

Augustine pointed out that an unborn fetus has eyes, ears, nose, mouth, hands, and feet but could not see, hear, smell, taste, grasp, or walk. Only after the babe was born could it use those tools. There was continuity from the life of the womb to life in the world, but also great differences. Similarly, that good bishop argued, there would be satisfying and fulfilling continuity between our lives before death and our lives after resurrection, but we can no more understand how than an unborn babe could understand what its existence would be like after it was born.

So we wait and see, either in fear or faith, or a healthy blend of both.

1. Immortality Denied

Don't tell my bishop: even though I'm an ordained Christian clergyperson, I don't believe in the immortality of the soul. I'm not even sure I believe there is such a thing as a soul.

Certainly I believe in all those characteristics of a human person that are attributed to a soul: personality, intelligence, memory, will power, self-awareness, and a sense of humor. I just don't believe that any of them has a separate existence that survives death. Don't tell my bishop.

Those mental activities that are associated with the soul are locked in with my physical being. I can't see without eyes, hear without eardrums, or taste without a tongue. If my hand is cut off, I can't feel without it. My perceptions are received by physical organs and interpreted by a physical organ; when the physical organs have ceased to be capable of biochemical reactions, how would a soul perceive things?

Same with memory. What happens to my memory after my biological organism stops functioning? Actually, my memory isn't doing that well while my cerebral neuron paths are still intact: I remember things I want to forget, and things I'd love to remember, although they're presumably still in storage somewhere between my ears, I cannot recover no matter how hard I try. How am I going to remember anything when the intracranial switchboard I've always depended on for memory loses its electrical power?

Medical evidence also undermines my attempts to keep my bishop happy by believing in the existence of a soul: lobotomies, removals of part of a person's gray matter, cause loss of memory or change of personality. As I understand it, the more gray matter removed the less memory and personality remain. But various theologies tell me, contrary to common sense, that when all the gray matter is rotten and inactive, suddenly my memory and personality spring to life outside the very medium they used to be so dependent on.

Clergy or not, I doubt it.

All those things science tells me my brain is doing – perception, memory, will – I certainly enjoy. But if I can't enjoy any of those things right now without a physical organism, I really don't understand how I'm going to enjoy them afterwards.

If you do report my agnosticism about immortality of the soul to my bishop, please remind him that the Bible doesn't say much about souls surviving death. In the one extensive case of life after death which the Bible claims to report there's nothing about a disembodied soul flitting around, just four accounts about somebody returning from the dead and eating bread and fish and being touched by friends. In fact, after his return from death, if the account is accurate, Jesus insists that he's not a spirit, or disembodied soul.

The Creator may, as scripture claims, love someone back into existence. The Power that brought me about in this time and space could just as easily bring me together again, fully reassembled, memories and all (in an improved version I would hope), in a new or different time and space. The possibility of eternal life by God's grace I can believe.

But not in an immortal soul. Don't tell my bishop.

2. New Age Responses

My bishop hasn't responded, as I feared he would, to the doubts – might be better to call them serious reservations – I expressed about the existence of an immortal soul. New Age folk, on the other hand responded more vehemently than anything I feared from any bishop.

Their attacks were often personal, what was called *ad hominem* back when Latin was in use. Some blamed me for the inquisition. Some blamed me for the holocaust. Some blamed me for the Republican Party. (I'm a Democrat; don't tell my bishop.) But none of them offered logical corrections to what they called my lame and distorted reasoning.

Many claimed that Christians, and in particular the clergy, of which I am one, are dreadfully old-fashioned and just don't know how to think properly or intelligently.

Charges of being old-fashioned from New Age folk that are serving warmed up leftovers from the fourth and fifth century neo-platonism of Plotinus and Porphyry? Hardly to be taken seriously.

Beyond the *ad hominem* attacks, however, there were two serious claims that deserve to be answered.

First, New Agers cited instances of something that had been in a previous body, like an Egyptian princess's, showing up in a modern body, like a Hollywood star's. (I'm not sure if this is a step up or a step down on the ladder of Karma.) In any case, when somebody in Kansas starts talking second millennium Coptic, the New Agers claim a soul has migrated.

I can accept their evidence. Not in most of the cases. But in some, yes, I'll grant a twentieth century person can remember something from a previous existence in the sixteenth, eighth, even first century. But how does that prove a soul? Those cases can just as easily be genetic survivals, physically linked.

Genetic material from one frog, trained to jump at the sound of a bell, can be inserted into another frog so that it too will remember to jump at a bell's sound. Why, then, can't memories from previous existences be passed along in some similarly quirky way in our DNA? I know the genes that make up my body and personality have been part of previous bodies in previous centuries. I don't know about a soul in my current body, let alone a previous one..

Isn't it awful for a clergyman to be so materialistically oriented?

Don't tell my bishop.

Second, New Agers cited examples of telekinesis or telepathy or clairvoyance to prove the existence of an immortal soul. Human minds have amazing powers, I don't deny it. They have powers to heal the body. Minds may have powers to move things at a distance. Minds may have powers to communicate across vast distances without sound. Minds may have powers to sense things at a distance, either in space or time. But these powers, if they exist, do not prove that minds can exist without bodies.

Worse part is: since I don't have any of these powers, it doesn't really matter to me if they do prove the soul's immortality. It just makes me very envious of all my friends and acquaintances who do have those powers with which they can reassure themselves about their continued existence after their electroencephalograms go flatline. (None of my friends, naturally, admit their powers to me, presumably for fear I become too jealous to maintain the friendship.)

I wonder if my bishop is telepathic.

3. Bible Thumpers' Responses

My bishop still hasn't heard about my doubting the immortality of the soul. All quiet on that front. But together with the deluge of letters from the New Age crowd I was inundated by complaints from a bunch of Bible thumpers.

Bible thumpers are distinguished from Bible readers. As a

clergyperson I bump into thumpers all the time. They think they know exactly what the Bible says about any issue: race relations, homosexuality, flower arrangements, and so on. But they don't. They just assume that the Bible supports their own positions. And when I ask them where the Bible actually says what they believe it says, they look at me blankly with no answer.

I play a game to identify thumpers. Whenever someone is holding forth noisily that the Bible opposes something like cloud seeding or supports something like rescheduling the first day of daylight saving, I always comment, "You must be referring to Hephaniah 2: 12."

Real Bible readers respond with a puzzled "No", but Bible thumpers look at my clergy collar, assume I know what I'm talking about even if they don't, and give a firm and unequivocal "Yes!"

I never pursue the discussion further. The Bible has no book of Hephaniah.

Thumpers wrote insisting that the Bible tells us there is an immortal soul. Some even pointed to a phrase either out of context or of variable interpretation, like the twenty-third Psalm's "Thou restorest my soul". I'm enough of a Hebrew student to know that means "You give my spirit a boost" and has nothing to do with immortality.

Use of the word "soul" in the Bible doesn't prove we have an immortal, nonphysical something-or-other in us any more than does the use of the word in a phrase like "soul music" (which I'd accept as a much better proof of immortality than any texts the Bible-thumpers could offer.)

Nowhere does the Bible say clearly "When a human dies, the soul leaves the body and the personality's self-awareness survives." I wish it did! Total annihilation is not a prospect I anticipate with relish.

Bible readers, as opposed to Bible thumpers, know that the Hebrew Bible, Genesis through Malachi, has very little about an after-life, that its few passages often contradict one another: some claim there is no existence after death, others that the after-life is only a shadowy, glum, and gloomy existence. No bright lights and happy reunions with earlier departees. This in a book that spans a thousand years of human experience! (Don't tell the New Age crowd.)

Christian books of the Bible have, of course, the Jesus story, which says nothing about the immortality of a soul but of the resurrection of a body. And Paul, who usually talks about resurrected bodies coming out of the ground, has in 1 Corinthians 15 something about spiritual bodies that always struck me as double talk. (Don't tell my bishop.)

My biggest difficulty is with the seance in 1 Samuel 28:8-19. I suspect it belongs in the same category as Jonah and the fish or the three lads in the furnace: not fact but legend or allegory or folk tale. But don't tell the thumpers. They believe the whole Bible is absolutely true even if they're not very clear exactly what the Bible says. And don't tell the New Age folk; they tend to believe in seances. But on this one at least, you can tell my bishop.

4. Resurrection

Somebody finally snitched to my bishop that I had denied the existence and immortality of the soul. I suspect it was some Bible thumper.

Actually, I hasten to point out, I didn't do a blatant denial so much as express minor doubts or polite reservations. Just raised a few questions is all I did. And before my defrocking commences, I'd like to clarify some aspects of what I said.

I never denied the possibility of life after death. (Tell my bishop.) I questioned that immortality of the soul is the means of life after death. Immortality of the soul is not a strong Biblical idea, and as a clergyperson I abide by my obligation to rely rather strongly on the Bible. (Tell my bishop.)

On a Biblical basis I was trying to give credit, responsibility, and an active role in life after death to God, who is even more important to me than my bishop. And the Bible, no matter what the thumpers claim, doesn't say we have immortal souls. It says God can raise people from the dead. The One who creates can also re-create.

Disregarding the Bible, my own experience is that I am a transitory and dependent creature, not eternal and independent. When I came into existence I wasn't aware or in control. All along the way between my birth and death are constant reminders that I'm not in full control and have the continual need to let go and to acknowledge and trust a higher power. I'm presupposing I'm not going to be aware or in control when I go out of existence either. The very difficult kind of letting go and trusting on a daily basis that I've had to practice all my life is what I'm going to have to do when I breathe my last.

On the other hand, believing in an immortal soul is easy. It's natural to presuppose that our mental activity goes on forever. The alternative is unthinkable. Literally. And in the face of the terrifying possibility that we're each rapidly approaching a time when we'll be totally obliterated it's so very comforting to believe that our consciousness will automatically survive and go on forever when our blood stops bringing oxygen to our brains. Immortality of the soul, if it were true, would be a natural and built-in feature; we wouldn't have to worry about life after death.

Probably I'm a natural born worrier. I worry about my congregation. I worry about aging. I worry, as you well know, about my bishop. And I worry, as my little essays have shown, that the whole idea of an immortal soul is merely wishful thinking or, as we used to say when Latin was in use, poppycock. (Actually I don't worry about immortal souls as much as about my bishop.)

Rather than alleviate my worries by believing that my self-awareness will automatically and naturally continue after all the rest of me stops, I console myself by trusting the Power that put me here in the first place to put me together again elsewhere and/or elsewhen. For my after-life I'm relying on a divine act from outside, not the existence of some kind of ectoplasmatic nebulosity inside me. My hope is based not on biology or psychology or pneumatology or whatever the relevant science is, but on theology.

Be sure to tell that to my bishop before my upcoming appointment with him. And I'll let you know how it goes.

5. Retraction, Maybe

Miracle! My bishop assigned me the penance of writing a retraction for my series of articles which questioned the existence of an immortal soul. This is a miracle because in my denomination, one of the many Protestant ones, the bishop has no authority to assign penance and, in fact, we don't even use the term "do penance". We leave penance to our Roman Catholic siblings. They do it so well.

But for obvious reasons (my bishop controls what parish I'm in) I want to keep my bishop happy, so here comes my retraction, affirming that it is, or at least may be possible to believe in the existence and immortality of the soul.

Various mental activities are usually considered aspects of an immortal "soul": perception, memory, emotions, self-awareness, and will power or the ability to choose. My argument was that things like perception, memory, and emotion all seem dependent on the physical organ, the brain. Change or remove part of the brain and you alter or eliminate sight, sound, taste, memories, and feelings. And if the whole brain stops functioning, the whole person presumably stops functioning.

Nothing survives.

My error might have been, now that my bishop insists I think it through, to lump self-awareness and will power in with memory, sense perception, and emotion. On reconsideration it may be that some sense of self-awareness survives after death. It would not, however, be self-awareness of memories. Memories are stored in cerebral circuitry that stops at death.

I don't like the idea that part of me may survive death but not my memories. But I'm stuck with it by the logic of my position.

If memories are gone, of what "self" does awareness survive once all the physical systems shut down? (This gets vague and hazy, but that's to be expected; theological anthropology is interpreting an obscurity by an uncertainty. St. Paul has his revenge.)

My bishop should appreciate a little parable to give a Biblical or churchy flavor to all this: Self-awareness or consciousness is like a non-physical executive power in our brains. It reads data provided to the brain by the sense organs. It sends directives from the brain to mouth and hands and legs to move. It runs through the filing system of memory to recover stories or pictures from the past. In all this it's always making choices among various options. It is in the brain but not of the brain.

When the brain dies, the executive loses the data input of the sense organs, limbs and organs to direct, and all the memory files. All that survives is awareness of the acquired skill of making choices.

What choices can be made after death without data input, limbs, or memories, I don't know. (I bet my bishop does!) But something – call it a soul if you want – can survive the termination of the organism and begin making a whole new set of self-aware choices in a totally different environment, like an executive leaving a familiar office for a new and strange one, but taking the basic administrative skills along and putting them to use in the new setting.

Having thought through this retraction, I must admit my bishop is very clever. He didn't point out my error about immortality of the soul; he left me to discover and correct it on my own. I just hope he's happy with my result. Actually, I'm not, but don't tell him. And cross your fingers my new parish won't be as bad as I fear.

6. Dante and Funerals

My bishop has pronounced absolution for me. And my college roommate from long years ago wrote to remind me about reading Dante together. Dante gives a helpful perspective on all those written reflections on the soul which wound up getting me assigned to a new parish. Well, not really new. Different. Actually old. Really old.

Dante, following a longstanding medieval tradition, depicted an afterlife which combined the Greek philosophical tradition of immortality of the soul with the scriptural tradition of resurrection of the body. In that picture at death the soul leaves the body and Greek philosophers are kept happy; at the final judgment the souls receive a body once again, Biblical scholars are happy together with those who composed the creed that says "in the resurrection of the body."

Ancient Greeks – brilliantly intuitive Plato, exhaustively thorough Aristotle, boisterously imaginative Aristophanes – had such active minds they just could not imagine their mental activity stopping at death. (Come to think of it, neither can we. It's impossible to imagine not imagining or to practice being aware of not being aware. Try it.) So they decided their mental activity survived beyond death: immortality of the soul.

Scripture writers, on the

other hand, wanted to give the Creator credit for everything, including life after death, so they portrayed the Creator as reconstituting the dead far off in the future. In the meantime, those who died no longer existed.

Medieval thinkers synthesized Greek immortality and scriptural resurrection by claiming that, first, the soul survived death in a natural way, and second, the person was resurrected or recreated by supernatural intervention way down the line.

Intellectually I'm not sure that the synthesis is an accurate description of what happens, but emotionally I love it because it gives me not one but two shots at going on forever. The more chances I get the happier I am.

Christian funeral services' presentation of these two different views serves as a practical and psychologically very sound means of consolation for the bereaved. In places the prayers speak of the deceased as still present or alive, as if the person's soul were flitting about. Those passages address and express the bereaveds' denial and reluctance to admit that the departed is in fact departed.

In other places Christian ceremonies speak of the deceased as dead and gone and waiting for a gift of renewed life ("ashes to ashes, dust to dust in sure and certain hope of resurrection . . ."). That addresses and expresses the bereaveds' acceptance of the loss and willingness to let go.

It's very reassuring for me to know that after my death my family and friends will be properly consoled by the Church's funeral ceremony. Their desire to hold on to me, to keep me alive, will be met by one set of images; their need to let go of me, to admit I no longer exist, will be helped by the other set of images.

But I'm still not sure after my death how I'm going to feel about it.

- - - - -

John Horan, editor of the *Northern Virginia Daily*, receives my special thanks for having "discovered" me and for having begun putting my editorials in print on a regular basis. I especially commend the courage of his willingness to publish essays whose tone and edge often have something to offend everyone: the pious and the skeptic, the liberal and the fundamentalist, the person in the pew and my bishop.

Actually, however, the first editorial of mine he published lacked the wit and bite some people claim they detect in my later material. "Dreadful Holidays," originally fell into place as a written piece to help Mildred Monza with her grief process after her husband's death.

"I'm dreading the holidays, Pastor," she had said.

As I talked with her about ways of coping I developed what would be the major themes of the article, which I wrote out both for her and for other members of my congregations who might seek similar advice and guidance. Envisioning a larger audience than Mildred and my own parishioners, I interwove suggestions and approaches for the Jewish community as well and had the resulting article declined by a wide variety of religious journals and family magazines. John Horan, bless him, finally picked it up for the *Northern Virginia Daily* in its current form, much abbreviated from its originally intended magazine article length.

That article launched my writing career with the *Northern Virginia Daily*. Although it was my first to appear, it is placed here, later in the anthology, because its tone is so different from my usual and expected style. I hope it somewhat repudiates my unfortunate reputation in some quarters as too often a sharp-tongued wise ass and presents a picture of me as able to be sympathetic and consoling. And please share copies with friends or family members to whom it may be some help as they grieve and face "the dreadful holidays".

- - - - -

Dreadful Holidays

"I'm dreading the holidays" is a common comment by those who have suffered a death in the family during the previous year. Loss and grief are keener in contrast to the joy and festivity of the season. Also, the daily absence of a spouse from the breakfast or dinner table gives daily practice for coping with that aspect of the loss, but the absence of a loved one from midnight mass or the family seder happens only once a year and consequently two contradictory feelings of people in grief need to be addressed. On the one hand is the wish that everything were the way it was before the death. A reflex of this wish is to keep the room or the bureau or the desk just the way it was and to follow the same patterns even if they no longer make sense.

On the other hand is a wish to avoid the pain and get past it all, which can inspire urges to travel, to sell the house, to break old ties and form new ones.

Healthy and helpful coping with the dreaded holidays acknowledges both of these tendencies and makes a conscious effort to walk a path between them, avoiding the extremes of "I want to do everything just the way we always did" and "I'm going to Arizona for the holidays so I don't have to face things at home."

Avoidance of facing the anxieties aroused at holidays often includes failure to do advance planning. This is like crossing dangerous terrain without a map because the thought of hidden quicksand or impenetrable jungle rouses fears. Better to face them on a map ahead of time than to be suddenly amid them unaware.

Plotting a course through the holidays begins with making an emotional map, a list of what will be hardest to face. A written list has the advantage of being tangible and concrete. Compiling the list as a family provides the support of having others share the burden of grief as well as make suggestions how to deal with it.

Good maps are always specific. The general observation "I'm dreading Christmas" isn't as much help in locating danger spots as concrete details: doing Christmas shopping, decorating the tree, going to services, sharing the family meal.

Some of these times will be more painful than others. It may be the departed family member didn't help with doing the shopping or decorating the tree. Although her or his absence will still be felt at those times, it won't be so keen. They can be anticipated as relatively safe zones.

Perhaps decorating the Christmas tree was always a special time. Between having the tree just as always and not having a tree at all, is there a way to acknowledge both loss and continuity? Decorate it as usual but put it in a different location? Use only half the decorations or decorate only one side?

Attend candlelight service as usual for continuity but sit in a different part of the church to acknowledge that this year things are different? Amid gift exchange give a gift either to one another or to a charity in memory of the deceased? Have the family dinner at the same house but change the menu, or have the same menu but at a different house.

Similarly at Passover in the spring it is better to redesign the seder in advance than to wait until all are at table and wonder how the readings will go without grandpop. Leave grandpop's chair empty as a reminder both of his presence and his absence? Have the chair empty at first, but then taken by the oldest son or offspring as acknowledgement that life and family traditions go on? Distribute the parts of the seder to different family members and have them each take grandpop's chair when they read?

Advance planning for holidays is naturally subject to revision even up to the last minute. The tree can be decorated just the way it always was or the family can decide to stay home from services. But intentional planning ahead of time means that some of the holidays' hurt and grief, experienced in advance by imagination, will not be as strong when the actual time comes. Also, the bereaved will have a sense of directions and bearings for moving through a difficult time. The holidays need not be dreaded as much when they are confronted beforehand.

- - - - -

Back in Virginia for a few months after an interim pastorate in Riegelsville and before starting one in Mechanicsburg, Pennsylvania, I responded with the following editorial to an announcement in the *Northern Virginia Daily* that a local group of witches had performed a public spell to help protect our troops in Afghanistan and that they were sponsoring a local Pagan Pride Day. Although some of my editorial anecdotes are pure fiction, the story included in this editorial about my leading worship with the Unitarian Universalists is wholly true.

- - - - -

The Bewitching Spell of Paganism
NVD September 3, 2004

Pagan spells with chanting, singing, drumming, and a crystal amulet to protect troops in Afghanistan? Count me in! But don't tell my bishop.

Hecate and Minerva! I've been praying for the protection of troops in Afghanistan and for world peace and cures for AIDS and cancer and a winning season for the Phillies for a long time now with very disappointing, in fact negligible, results.

I try formal prayers: "Almighty and most merciful God, from the storehouse of your abundant grace, vouchsafe to bestow upon us ..."

I try informal prayers: "Sweet Jesus, I just want to lift up to you this burden in my heart about . . ."

Nothing!

Maybe it's time I pitch in with the pagans – though only occasionally since my vocation as a Lutheran pastor is what puts bread on my table. Wonder if the pagan tradition has spells for turning stones to bread or multiplying loaves and fishes? My tradition lays claim to those kinds of things but alas! they're part of the secrets of my tradition that they never taught us in seminary.

So let me gather at the river with wiccans, wizards, witches, and whichevers to add my energy to their energy in weaving a spell for harmony and peace.

People together can, I know, generate a lot of energy. Just mention ordaining gays or lesbians among a group of Lutherans and watch the energy level go way up. Among a group? Hey, just two people are enough! The problem is that all that fantastic energy is dissipated because of the polarization of the group, or the two people, into positives and negatives that cancel each other out. But get a group together focusing their energy on world peace and something's likely to happen.

Alas again! It's been my experience that it's much easier to get people together to waste their energy on a divisive issue like a marriage amendment than it is to gather them to focus their energy on something they all agree on like world peace.

Pagan spells, like the local one used recently for troops in Afghanistan, often involve precious gems or stones. And precious gems and stones do, I know, help focus energy and make things happen. I know that apart from what I have read in "De Lapidibus," a book on the power of gems and stones by Albert the Great, the teacher of no less a scholar than Thomas Aquinas, the premiere Roman Catholic theologian. I know from my own experience how much power can be wielded by a diamond, emerald, or ruby, especially if it's set in a box that says Tiffany's. It can make all kinds of unexpected things happen.

Local pagans do, in some ways, I must admit, have me puzzled. I'm not sure how those who believe in a multiplicity of gods and goddesses fit in with Unitarians, whose very name declares that they believe in the unity of only one God in distinction from us crazy Trinitarian Christians who can't decide if God is three or one.

And I'm puzzled how welcome I'd be among pagan Unitarians. Two years ago I led a Sunday solstice celebration at the local Unitarian Universalist Sunday gathering. (My bishop already knows; maybe that's why he hasn't placed me with a congregation!) I lit the chalice of unity with the rays of the sun through a Fresnel lens and used good ol' pagan Plato as one of my texts. But I heard that some members stayed away because they didn't want to associate with one of them thar Trinitarian Christians in spite of all their talk about all creeds being welcome. I guess there are weak links in all religious chains.

In any case, I'll probably wander among the displays on Pagan Pride Day, wearing my clergy collar and looking to see if any of the Pagans try to ward me off with the sign of the cross … I mean the pentacle. I just wish as a sign of peace, good will, and shared goals some of the local churches would join me and pitch in with their own stands and displays in support of the "pagan" goals of harmony with nature and peace among humanity.

- - - - -

Having finished the interim pastorate in Mechanicsburg, Pennsylvania, on September 30, 2005, I returned to Virginia. Previously I had submitted editorials to the *Northern Virginia Daily* irregularly as the spirit (Spirit?) moved me. I decided to get serious, not about the content of my articles but about their regularity. As a personal discipline I started writing and submitting two articles every week. John Horan did not give me my own column, "Altar Ego Musings," as I had suggested to him, but he was very gracious and faithful in picking up my material for op-ed publication. Those which were published after my return to Virginia begin here; the ones he decided not to use I may publish in a separate volume entitled *Left Behind*.

The first in that series is about atheists, and was in some ways a response to an ongoing battle in the *Northern Virginia Daily's* letters to the editor between some evangelical atheist humanists and members of the religious community. Further editorials bouncing off of that epistolary conflict follow later.

- - - - -

When Atheists Pray
November 3, 2005

"How would atheist children handle school prayer if it returns?" I mused. Atheists don't pray.

Or do they? I mused further.

In a dark and secluded alley late at night, approached by three burley figures obviously intent on mugging, a person is likely to yell "Help!" even if there seems no one behind the darkened apartment windows to hear it.

From deep inside the most faithful atheist must arise a similar cry after hearing bad news: an operation and biopsy are needed or receiving a pink slip with the paycheck or realizing that the ammunition is about to run out and the enemy is still relentlessly pushing in.

Atheists faithfully believe there's no one there to hear, but on occasion they yell just the same.

I don't believe the old adage that there are no atheists in fox holes. I respect atheists and their convictions. I don't think they give up on their convictions just because they think the next assault wave will be fatal. Atheists are in foxholes. Their psyches scream to the cosmos "Help!" as loudly as the theists'. They wrestle, however, with the frustration of believing there is no one there to hear them.

Similarly, an atheist's heart must almost automatically well full with gratitude, with a sense of thankfulness, at exceptionally beautiful sunrises or magnificent starlit nights or the doctor's report "It was benign" or the sound of back-up troops and supplies pulling in. Deep inside the atheist, something expresses an inarticulate "Thank you!" The atheist thinks no one is aware of this sense of gratitude, no one overhears this inarticulate "Thank you." Theists, of course, would claim the atheist is heard by a god, or, depending on the nature of the theism, gods or goddess(es). Atheists can pray without knowing it.

Musing on this, I began to muse about school prayer. I'm opposed to it even though I'm an ordained Lutheran clergyperson. There are all kinds of theological, sociological, and constitutional reasons for my stance. But behind those is my deep-seated conviction that no one can lead a public prayer as well as I can so why should anyone bother?

And if I were asked to lead public prayer in school, what would I say, realizing the crowd in front of me included Lutherans and Baptists, Jehovah's Witnesses and Rastiferians, Muslims and Hindus, and, of course, atheists?

I'd say "We're grateful for . . ." with particular fill ins: "for this new day . . . for our freedoms as Americans . . . for the opportunity today to vote . . . for the coming vacation . . . for our teachers and staff . . ." etc. No need to address the "thank you" to Allah or Krishna, Jesus or Jehovah. Let those saying it mentally address it to their particular favorite; let the atheists just express the sentiment but cling to their assumption that nobody is there to listen. (Of course the Pessimist Society will object "Why be grateful for a new day? All a new day means is more trouble! Why for an opportunity to vote? The wrong candidate will surely win. Etc.")

"We are concerned," I would say before the class, "About the victims of Hurricane Katrina; we want them helped." Who would object? Children who belong to a Wicca would know they were talking to Gaea or Hecate; atheist children would know they were just expressing a concern and wish – and make a mental note to remind their parents to supplement donations of church goers by giving generously to Katrina relief funds since there is no God to intervene.

Religious children could be

content to know each was addressing the only real god or goddess there is – their own; atheist children would know anyone was foolish who thought some Being actually heard these noble sentiments, but they would share them nonetheless. Everybody would be satisfied. Except, maybe, the Pessimist Society. (For "prayers" written to order, bohmhome@shentel.net.)

- - - - -

The writers of letters to the editor from the religious community were always so self-assured and confident in their own opinions that they seemed unwilling even to try other ideas on for size. And one of the atheist letter writers identified a website that asserts Jesus never existed. The tension between those two poles of absolute certainty and extreme skepticism produced, among others, the following editorial.

- - - - -

The Virtue of Skepticism
NVD November 9, 2005

"Jesus didn't exist" brings up interesting internet sites when it's entered in a search engine.

Some are about a film "The Beast," based on the assumption that Jesus was a fabrication and never existed. It's scheduled for release at the beginning of next June, 6/6/'6 to be exact. But probably as a Christian clergyperson I shouldn't help promote it by mentioning it. Don't tell my bishop!

Most of the websites argue, however, that the evidence for the existence of Jesus is too slim to be taken seriously. The four official records of Jesus' life, it's claimed, were obviously written by believers with a deep commitment and therefore cannot be trusted as objective, unbiased accounts but must be dismissed.

Suetonius and Tacitus composed their histories of Rome in the second century and so were thus not eye-witnesses of Jesus. Older sources which they used for their reports on the 64 C.E. fire in Rome for which Christians were blamed may not have been accurate and there's no way to determine their reliability.

Josephus, the Jewish historian and Roman sympathizer, wrote in the second half of the first century. Some manuscripts of his history of the Jewish people have passages about Jesus. Were they in his original, or were they later insertions or emendations by a monk, well intentioned but ignorant of twentieth century rules of historiography?

How is the "evidence" evaluated?

Similarly, the recent political campaigns provided facts, information, and interpretations, all as evidence for believing, trusting, and voting for one person. Or, given much of the recent campaign, for voting against his or her opponent.

Evidence always needs to be evaluated, whether then or now, whether written or oral, and I'm on the side of the patron saint of skeptics, the apostle Thomas who didn't take his fellow apostles' word for the resurrection of Jesus and thus earned the nickname "Doubting." Like him, I don't simply accept without questioning the account in the newspaper, the testimony of the politician, the report by Josephus, or even any of the Gospels.

Evaluating evidence means asking questions. What other evidence is there? What problems might there be in the evidence? When one set of evidence is contradicted by another set, how is the truth determined? What bias is there in the sources of the evidence, whether written or spoken?

Questioning the bias of a writer or reporter means I also have to question my own biases. Am I believing one set of evidence because I already lean in that direction and want to believe it? Or am I to the best of my ability being fair and impartial? Do I believe one politician or political party statement simply because I'm sympathetic to that party? Do I believe the gospels simply because I'm a Christian?

Trying to be fair and impartial is an excellent exercise in humility and understanding. The humility comes from willingness to entertain the notion that we might be wrong: that the politician from the party we never trust might in fact be right, that the atheist, or Christian, might be right. And naturally stretching our imaginations to try to see things from a perspective different from our own deepens and strengthens our understanding of others, whether we wind up agreeing with them or not.

Evaluating evidence by asking questions is a process of tracking down the truth, not making judgments on the assumption, somewhat arrogant, that we already know or have the truth and therefore don't really need to participate in a dialogue or debate.

Dialogue and debate in an effort to arrive at the truth, however are unfortunately not popular modes of discourse. (Maybe political spin doctors have made us so skeptical of arriving at the truth that we're no longer willing even to try.) Too many would rather talk – even shout – than listen, rather be certain of their opinions than wrestle with the presentation of other facts, rather be comfortable than face the possibility of having to change their minds or allegiances. Probably, as often, the truth – in politics or Religion – lies in the middle ground and not at the noisy, argumentative extremes. (Further discussion welcome at: bohmhome@shentel.net)

- - - - -

"How is Scripture properly used?" became the theme of a number of editorials in the fall of 2005. The first one reflects on the use of the Bible as a model, or not, of political procedures.

- - - - -

Undemocratic Scripture
NVD November 16, 2005

Democracy does not have a strong Biblical foundation. Sacred scripture does not support our revered American process of using a voting to decide what is right or wrong, at least legally if not morally. In Holy Writ the majority does not rule; God does. Instead of by means of "All in favor . . . All opposed," decisions are made or leaders chosen by means of an uncompromising "Thus saith the Lord."

Departure from Egypt was not the result of a poll taken while the Hebrew people were building for the Pharaoh. God sent Moses to confront Egypt's existing power structure, set the people free, and lead them out.

Presumably the people of Israel concurred with the divine decision. But not for long. A vote actually was taken at Numbers 14:1-4: "All the people raised a loud cry . . . They said to one another, 'Let us choose a captain and go back to Egypt.'" But popular opinion does not determine divine policy; God threatened pestilence and disinheritance. And on the people went for forty more years.

Jesus' disciples in effect voted unanimously not to go to Jerusalem to celebrate the Passover because they anticipated resistance and hostility from the religious leaders. (John 11:8) But in spite of the majority vote, Jesus said "Let's go" and on they went.

America's religious right, which one bumper sticker claims is neither, is strongly imbued with this sense of indifference to what the majority wants; they are concerned only about what their Divinity wants as they perceive it.

God has said no to homosexuality? (Leviticus 20:13) The religious right resists gay marriages. God has said no to weaving together two different materials in one garment? (Leviticus 19:19) The religious right pushes the enforcement of that restriction on the fabric industry. God has said no to eating pork or shrimp or lobster? (Leviticus 20:25; 11:7, 10) . . . Well, the religious right doesn't insist that all the rabbinic count of 613 Hebrew Bible commandments are still in effect. The Holy Spirit is gracious enough to inform true Bible believers which divine mandates still apply, which do no longer.

As usually happens in Scripture, a movement in one direction has a counter movement. Passages insisting on Jewish exclusivism have their corrective balance in passages that declare Judaism's eventual universality. Paul's emphasis on the irrelevance of good works is countered by James' emphasis on doing good works. And for all the autocratic, monarchical, even despotic tendency of the Bible there is nonetheless a counter movement of democratic action.

Abraham voted against God's own decision to destroy Sodom and Gomorrah. (Genesis 18:2-33) and without threats of pestilence or disinheritance God agreed to a compromise.

Israel's majority voted to have a king. God voted against. But the majority carried the day and God went along with the majority, though not without muttering "You'll be sorry!" (1 Samuel 8)

God was allowed (Acts 1:23-26) to chose which disciple would replace Judas, but only after the disciples had already voted and limited God's choice only to either Matthias or Joseph Justus. The disciples "cast lots," like drawing straws, between the two, trusting that God was manipulating the results. One wonders how God felt if neither of those two had been the Divine Majesty's own choice.

(When two political candidates are within say, three per cent of one another after an election, or if the election is, as sometimes happens, hotly contested with calls for a recount, maybe this same Biblical approach could be used. Let straws be drawn! The outcome can then be credited to or blamed on God or, for atheists, the twin Ladies Luck: Good and Bad. Save wear and tear of the electoral process!)

God didn't even get a chance to vote at a major meeting in the early church to decide how many of the commandments needed to be kept by converts from paganism. After debate, James reached a decision that only a few laws need be kept, and all agreed. God didn't even have a chance to draw straws. And unfortunately the list of "keepers" hasn't survived in detail; presumably prohibitions against pork, shrimp, and lobster are no longer in effect, but those against homosexuality still are.

For all God's autocratic tendencies in scripture, it seems the Creator can nevertheless be a team player and go along with a majority vote. (Cast your vote at bohmhome@shentel.net)

- - - - -

Not always beating the drum about what I consider proper use of the Bible, I varied the pace with this holiday peace.

- - - - -

Thanks for Creation
NVD November 19, 2005

Thanksgiving's approach reminds me what an ingrate I am. Well, maybe not an ingrate, but definitely out of synch with many – most? – of my religious friends and associates. When they're asked in a church or religious context to give thanks for "the good things of creation" they usually respond in terms of earth and sea, plants and trees, moon and stars, birds and animals. I suspect they're being strongly influenced by the catalogue of "the basic building blocks of creation" in the first chapter of the Bible's first book.

I do enjoy and am grateful for those things and I do offer appropriate prayers on my frequent walks through the woods or during nighttime sessions with my telescope or while brushing my cat. But for me, spoiled as I have been by school systems some inaccurately call "godless," "the good things of creation" calls up for me the mysterious and intriguing population of subatomic particles and the varied inhabitants of the Periodic Table, the Red Giants and White Dwarfs not of fairyland but of deep space, quasars and black holes, measurements by light years and the Doppler shifted, distant galaxies – realties often and unfortunately ignored in the language of the Church.

Church language and the language of everyday life, for instance on television or in the board room, are in fact often out of synch. Sometimes that's good: where everyday life hears talks about competition and winning, the Church talks about cooperation and helpfulness; where the world talks about getting even, the Church talks about forgiveness; where the world claims it doesn't exist if you can't touch it or measure it, the Church talks about God and angels, grace and goodness.

But I wish more of the language and concepts of the twenty-first century had found their way into the pews and pulpits so that I wouldn't feel so out of synch.

Indeed some hymns with more contemporary language about creation than stars, trees, and animals have wandered even into our "new" Lutheran hymnal – "new" as of thirty years ago, although still considered too avant garde by some of our congregations. "Loud boiling test tubes, sing to the Lord a new song." "Lord of the atom, we praise your might." A hymn for Christ's ascension runs "And have the bright immensities Received our risen Lord Where light-years frame the Pleiades" and address him as "Lord of interstellar space."

Such hymns with terms not found in the Bible may not sit well with those believers who reject evolution even as a viable theory and who insist that our planet is only six thousand years. Those folk are likely also to reject language from other parts of modern science's pictures of creation: electrons and muons, quarks and neutrinos as basic constituents of all things, neutron stars and cosmic rays, photons and dark matter. But those of us who are grateful to the Creator for those intricate and necessary subtleties welcome chances to mention them with thanks at the Divine Throne.

Talk about out of synch with thanksgiving language! Several Novembers ago I was in a prayer circle and the leader invited us first to name people for whom we were grateful. Next, things for which we were grateful to God for having created. At that point naturally parts of the Genesis catalogue were dutifully mentioned. Thinking of the Genesis stories myself, I gratefully blurted out "Sex!"

Such unbelieving stares I got from the other believers! (Send your own thanksgiving petitions to: bohmhome@shentel.net.)

- - - - -

After Thanksgiving I returned to the theme of proper use of the Bible with an editorial that was an abbreviation of a Bible study I had developed and used in a number of congregations. It had the same title, "Biblical Family Values," and ranged from exploring the polygamy and acceptance of incest in the early Hebrew Bible to the stress on celibacy in the Christian books of scripture.

- - - - -

Biblical Family Values
NVD December 3, 2005

"Traditional Biblical Family Values" as appealed to by some folks are certainly at variance with the family values that I find in my Bible.

To be sure, in the harmonious and peaceful Garden of Genesis (Genesis 2:24) before humanity was exiled into the harsh and lawless wilderness, the ideal of a union of one man and one woman was clearly established. Of course, it had to be that way; there were only one man and one woman.

But after the exile and population growth, look out!

Abraham's wife, without any indication of subsequent divine displeasure, lent her serving girl to her husband to beget children. Presumably Abraham agreed only as a matter of fulfilling a duty and didn't actually get any pleasure from his role in the begetting process. My Bible has this at Genesis 16:2. Presumably it isn't committing adultery or being unfaithful if the wife is complicit and encourages the relationship. Interesting family values!

Their grandson, Jacob, renamed Israel, had two wives, Rachel and Leah, who each gave their serving girls, Bilhah and Zilpah, to Jacob "as a wife." (Genesis 30:3, 9) Leah even hired Jacob from Rachel for a night of love-making. The son of his union was named Issachar, a pun on "Hire" in Hebrew. (Genesis 30:14-18) Interesting family values.

My Bible also reports that Solomon, the third king of Israel and builder of the temple in Jerusalem, had "among his wives seven hundred princesses and three hundred concubines." These were presumably for the sake of political alliances and Solomon didn't have sexual relationships with them, or, if he did, like Abraham he didn't really enjoy it. Maybe political leaders had special compensations from normal moral expectations. They often do! Or maybe they were the only ones who could afford polygyny. Either way, interesting family values!

One of the 613 commandments, by the traditional rabbinic count, required a man to have sexual relations with the widow of his dead brother. (Deuteronomy 25:5) Apparently this law was in effect before Sinai and the commandments because

Tamar was very disappointed when her brother-in-law, Onan, filled in, as it were, inadequately for her late husband Er. So she seduced her father-in-law, Judah. Judah even compliments her on the deception. (Genesis 38) Interesting family values.

Jesus didn't propose changes to the law that a man was expected to have intercourse with his dead brother's widow when he was asked a question relevant to it (Matthew 22:25-30). He did, however, encourage celibacy. I think. My Bible isn't clear. It reports Jesus as saying "Some make themselves eunuchs for the sake of the Kingdom of Heaven." (Matthew 19:12) I take that figuratively to mean that some practice celibacy, like most of the current Roman Catholic priesthood, to be unencumbered by wife and children and free to do the work of the Kingdom. Fundamentalists are welcome to take the saying literally, as the fourth century theologian, Origen, did and castrated himself.

Supporting the figurative interpretation of Jesus' eunuch saying, both Paul and John also encouraged celibacy. 1 Corinthians 7:8 says it is well to remain unmarried – quite a contrast to having seven hundred wives – and Revelation 14:4 reports a special place in heaven for "those who have not defiled themselves with women for they are virgins."

From uncontested polygamy and encouragement of an abundance of (male!) children in earlier Bible times, the "traditional values" shift around Jesus time to celibacy and virginity. In the Bible's two thousand year time span "family values" undergo a process of evolution. Excuse me! I mean "process of change." And I'm never sure which of the varied traditions is intended by those who appeal to "traditional family values in the Bible." Maybe I'm using the wrong Bible. (Suggestions for a different Bible are welcome at bohmhome@shentel.net)

One of my earliest published editorials was "Late for Christmas." I had so much enjoyed that one and its sequel, "Christmas: No Silent Night" that I was afraid I'd never again be able to write another Christmas editorial. Fortunately I was wrong, as the following editorials show . . .

- - - - -

Christmas Clutter
NVD December 10, 2005

Christmas season has gotten cluttered up with all kinds of things that have nothing to do with the birth of a special baby in Bethlehem a few millennia ago. That used to irritate me.

What do snowmen – I mean snow people – talking or otherwise, and reindeer, red-nosed or otherwise, have to do with Jesus' birth in a land that has neither snow nor reindeer?

Strings upon strings of colored lights and illuminated figurines cover lawn after lawn in an extravagant abundance, sometimes with a crèche off in a corner behind Santa and Rudolph, but even more often without.

How I used to fuss! Mistletoe and decorated evergreen trees from the Druid tradition! Lengthy garlands of ivy. Ivy traditionally sacred not to Jesus but to the Greek god Dionysus . . . To Dionysus . . .

Recalling Dionysus, however, set me musing.

"What has that to do with Jesus?" I was asking about all the extravagant and extraneous accretions to the Church's Festival of the Nativity. In the same way ancient Greeks used to ask "What has that to do with Dionysus?" at some of the earlier plays in the later tradition of Aeschylus and Sophocles, Euripides and Aristophanes. Athenian tragedy and comedy began in religious pageantry about Dionysus but evolved – I mean "developed" – far beyond their origin and any mention of Dionysus.

Imagine adding a little drummer boy to a traditional Christmas pageant and then, after a few decades, having a Christmas pageant, not about Jesus' birth and with no mention of Jesus, but exclusively about the little drummer boy after he'd grown up. And imagine eventually having at Christmas time just very powerful dramas with no connection to the Jesus story at all.

That imaginary account is similar to the actual history of those powerful Greek dramas about Orestes and Oedipus, Antigone and Electra, which have survived twenty four centuries without any mention of Dionysus for whose festival they were produced. *Oedipus* may have nothing to do with Dionysus, but what a story! Lysistrata's sex strike might even run counter to Dionysian extravagant sexuality, but what a story! That comparison set me musing further.

Maybe all the exuberance and spectacle, the strings of colored lights and voices of Nat King Cole and Frank Sinatra blaring through loudspeakers, the din of the Salvation Army bell and the blinkin' glare of the blue light special, even if not specifically related to Jesus' birth, are nonetheless an excellent thing. The whole world parties!

I mused about how the baby born in Bethlehem, when he grew up, loved a party! His opponents accused him to his disciples of being "A glutton and a drunkard, a friend of tax collectors and sinners." One of his favorite parables for the Kingdom of God (Matt. 22: 1; Luke 14: 16, etc.) was a feast or banquet, presumably a big party with good wine (John 2:10), lots of lights (Matthew 25:7), dancing, and festivity.

He claimed to be with us so that people could "have life, and have it more abundantly." (John 10:10) Sure enough, at the time of year when some people, though to be sure not all, focus on his birth there is an abundance of life: vitality, celebration, festivity!

Knowing the occasion of his arrival prompts people to party would be (or is, depending on your view of the resurrection) a source of pleasure to him, I'm sure. He must rejoice that as a result of his birth Republicans and Democrats exchange cards, even if the picture on it is a tipsy mouse in a cocktail glass rather than a manger scene. Tax collectors and sinners, atheists and witches, Kaine and Kilgore, secular humanists and fundamentalists – well, many fundamentalists – (some?) – all get along a little better and share a sense of wonderful camaraderie and cheer amid all of Christmas's clutter, both religious and secular.

That grownup babe is probably glad that Rudolph was finally reconciled with those who used to laugh and call him names, even if they don't make the sign of the cross before launching into the sky in front of the sleigh. He probably rejoices in the merriment of the children chasing Frosty down to the village square even if neither Frosty nor they were ever baptized in his name.

Unknown and invisible behind the scenes, even unmentioned and unacknowledged, God's powerful and creative Word, which some believe took flesh in Jesus of Nazareth, still inspires humanity to reconcile, celebrate, and party. Merry Christmas! (Send Christmas greetings to: bohmhome@shentel.net)

- - - - -

The following editorial is a fraud. Pretending to be a topical piece for Christmas season, it actually is another attempt, like my article on purgatory, to interpret a Roman Catholic practice in ways in which Protestants may be able to understand it.

- - - - -

Marley's Ghost
NVD December 5, 2005

Marley's ghost, making his seasonal reappearances to Ebenezer Scrooge, has me musing about contacts and communications with the dead.

Popular culture shows strong curiosity, if not interest in the possibility of crossing the barrier between the living and the dead. The theme is fascinating enough to sell movies like Patrick Swayze's *Ghost* and Bruce Willis' *Sixth Sense* and to support television series like *Dead Zone*, Edwards' *Crossing Over*, and *Medium*. Society is also increasingly interested in things like channeling or reading Tarot cards or crystals or performances of séances by spiritual advisors.

Talking to the departed is not an unusual practice for the majority of the world's Christian believers. One third of them, the Orthodox churches, as well as the Roman Catholic Church regularly greet Jesus' mother with "Hail, Mary!" or bid Peter, Andrew, James, or John, "Pray for us."

Protestants Christians, like

my own Lutheran denomination, don't usually talk to the dead, or, to use the official jargon, "invoke the saints." But even if our theology is agin' it, I sometimes do it anyway. Reading a majestic Latin hymn by Ambrose of Milan or singing a rousing hymn by Isaac Watts I whisper to them a sincere "Thank you!" Don't tell my bishop!

Christians, even Lutherans, regularly ask one another to pray for them. Congregations formally in the Sunday service and prayer circles informally during the week pray for those with special needs. If Tilly Schmaltzreid has been prayed for by the congregation, I'm sure once she has departed to the throne of grace she will return the favor and commend the congregation and her family and friends to the One on the throne. That is, she'll pray for them. Unless, of course she's miffed with them because their prayers for her healing weren't answered in quite the way she wanted.

Figure, if I could ask my brother while he was alive to pray for me, why stop asking him now just because he's dead. I mean, "departed." Can I be sure he hears me? Of course not! But then I often couldn't be sure he heard me while he was alive and that didn't stop me from asking. Can I be sure Ambrose, Isaac Watts, Mary, Antony, or Jude hear me? No. Can I be sure they can't hear me? Also no.

If indeed those who have "crossed over,' to use the newer jargon, might be able to hear us, why not ask them for help? Not just that they should pray to the Creator for us from their heavenly residence, but that they should help us out in some concrete way. Worth a try!

Or maybe not.

St. Antony of Padua is the one invoked in Roman Catholic tradition to help recover lost property or find lost objects. Hoping he's not aware I'm Lutheran, I often asked for his help because I often misplace things. Sometimes he seemed to help, sometimes he didn't. I must admit, though, the frequency of his helping me was slightly higher than my brother's had been when he was alive.

My car keys were missing. "Saint Antony, give aid" seemed more profitable to mutter than "Where'd I leave the damn things?" And immediately the thought occurred to me "Get down and look under the serving table." I looked. The keys were not there. Getting back up I whacked my head a good one.

Maybe St. Antony was/is a practical joker. Or maybe the

idea didn't come into my head from St. Antony. Maybe it was put there by some malevolent spirit that overheard my request and enjoys setting up situations that are likely to result in human suffering.

There's the problem. Talking to someone 'beyond the veil,' you don't know who is listening or who is responding. If there are spiritual entities like ghosts, there can also be malicious or evil spiritual entities out there ready to imitate St. Antony or my brother to my harm or detriment. Neither the power operating the Ouija Board from the "other side" nor the vision appearing to the medium can be trusted.

It seems to me much safer to talk to the departed than to listen to them, to say "Mark, this congregation bears your name; ask the Divine Majesty to kick their . . . I mean to straighten them out" or "Clive Staples, that was a wonderful novel; thank you!" or "Oh Jack, my dear brother; I don't know which stock to use for my pension."

Of course I wouldn't have trusted him much on a response to that one even when he was still alive. (Communications from living or dead: bohmhome@shentel.net)

- - - - -

Sometimes the Northern Virginia Daily printed the title for an article that I had suggested. Sometimes they replaced my suggestion with one much worse. For the editorial about sex in heaven, for example, they used "Sex a Risky Topic for Clergy" instead of my choice, "Heavenly Sex." The following they entitled "Beware of Santa Claus." I prefer the pun of my original title: "Beware of Claus" . . . and teeth and nails and pointy tail.

- - - - -

Beware of Claus
NVD December 21, 2005

Boycott Hallowe'en, recommend some Christian believers, claiming its practices are survivals of ceremonies for the dead, which is true, and a form of honoring or worshipping Satan, which I doubt. Any spiritual power who feels his honor and reputation are enhanced by children prowling the streets dressed as mutant ninja turtles or sticking their heads in water troughs filled with apples is hardly a dark force to be reckoned with. If anything, I'd think Hallowe'en foolishness and nonsense deride and mock the Evil One more than flatter and serve him.

Luther himself, in whose heritage I serve as pastor, did say the thing Satan hated most was being laughed at. Old Nick wants to be taken with deadly seriousness as a fierce Sovereign, not held up to ridicule by inconsequential frivolity and childish fakery.

Possible vestiges in Hallowe'en festivities of Satanism, witchcraft, and demon worship, however, did set me to musing about some of the fringe trappings of society's celebration of Jesus' birth. Fringe? Rapidly moving to the center! The more I thought about it the more alarmed I became by the subtle incursion into the season of Christ's Nativity by the One who beguiled and misled Adam and Eve in the guise of a serpent.

Has anyone noticed how in just the past century and a half Santa Claus has inveigled his way into the holiday?

Never mind boycotting Hallowe'en, I say; boycott Santa Claus instead!

Before I make my case that our modern Santa Claus is an incarnation of Satan, let me assure readers that my seminary did instruct me all about Santa's prototype, Saint Nicholas, the fourth century Bishop of Myra in Asia Minor, modern Turkey. He was well known for his charity to the poor; one legend reports that he once threw three bags of gold over a garden wall to provide dowries to three poor maidens. And so he came to be associated with one of the season's phenomena: gift giving.

But in medieval stained glass windows and renaissance art St. Nicolas is slender and wears dark earth colors, not fat and wearing a bright red suit. There's been a serious transformation. As in the serpent in the garden, now the Devil appears in the guise of Santa Claus, encouraging greed and selfishness.

Red suit, did I say? Who else is traditionally depicted in a bright red outfit? Not only can the Devil not change his hoof, as the saying goes, but, bold and brazen, he doesn't even bother to change clothing.

Some scholars have suggested that Santa's peaked hat is a corrupt survival of the bishop's erect miter which Nicolas would have worn, but now flaccid and flopped over as a sign of the church's impotence in the face of Evil. Perhaps so, but perhaps also that's just an overreaction by others who, like me, have sensed the danger and are sounding the alarm.

But consider further. What kind of creatures make their rounds at midnight? And where does the Figure in scarlet come from? He arrives, appropriately enough, out of the fiery place, out of the place of flames. What could be more obvious?

Think of the name. "Santa" is a form of a word for "Saint." But we don't call Santa Barbara "Santa," we call her Barbara; San Francisco isn't known as "San;" he's Francisco or Francis. Santo Domingo? Domingo or Dominic, never Santo! But Nicolas, abbreviated to "Claus," regularly goes by Santa. Devilishly subtle! It's an acronym, a rearranged spelling, of Satan! And for decades he's gotten away with it and no one has noticed.

Consider also "Jolly old Saint Nick." For whom is Old Nick a nickname?

Pardon my skepticism about a popular figure in popular culture. But consider this. How would a policeman normally respond if a fat and hairy, garishly dressed stranger invited children to sit on his lap and whispered into their ears, "Are you good? And what can Santa give *you* for Christmas?"

The Prince of Darkness, it's said, can disguise himself as an angel of light. Why not also as a jolly adaptation of a Christian saint? Beware!

Hues and cries are likely to result from my analysis, accusation, and warning. Let the very vehemence of Santa's defenders be a clear sign of how strong and inordinate a grip he has gained on the popular imagination. Almost as if people were under a spell! The situation is much worse than the minor enchantments of Hallowe'en and it needs to be dealt with. I may be called an old Scrooge, but it's eminently untrue! I am not really very old.

- - - - -

For a year in the nineties I filled in and did some supplementary teaching for the Institute for Jewish-Christian Understanding at Muhlenberg College. When the new director arrived and settled in he had what I thought were some excellent suggestions for intentional ways to emphasize Christianity's roots in the Jewish faith. He didn't go so far as the following suggestion. But I did.

Christian Chanukah
NVD 2006

Channukah... er, that is Hanukkah – I mean Hannukah – Chan... – in any case, the Jewish Festival of Lights should be observed by Christians even if we can't spell it accurately! Like Abraham and Sarah, Moses and Miriam, David and Bathsheba, Daniel and the lion, Esther and Ahasuer... Ahaseur... Ahas... King Xerxes (Esther 1:1), it's part of our Jewish heritage.

Because, however, the story of Chan... of that festival isn't reported in the main part of the Bible we share with our Jewish neighbors, it hasn't become one of those stories told and retold in our Sunday Schools or parochial schools. It's told in the books of the Maccabees, which narrate events after the Jewish return from exile in Babylon and before the birth of the prophet from Nazareth to Mary and Joseph. The books of the Maccabees join other "apocryphal" books like Judith and the Wisdom of Solomon, Tobit and Daniel versus the Priests of Baal, possibly the oldest surviving mystery short story. All of these the Church and Synagogue consider important material, but not quite on the same special level as Genesis, Exodus, and Leviticus or Matthew, Mark, and Luke.

Rejoice to learn you needn't read all of the Maccabees to know the story of Hann... of what the Maccabees did. Many newspapers at this time of year as a gesture of religious good will report on the festival and summarize the history of the Jewish rebellion, led by Judas Maccabee, against the oppressive attempts to wipe out Jewish traditions and practice by the Syrian overlord, Antiochus, nicknamed Epiphanius because he wanted to be considered an epiphany, or manifestation, of Zeus.

Chanukkah itself, those newspaper articles will report, means "Dedication" and recalls the Rededication of the Jerusalem Temple after it had been desecrated by Antiochus and made over to the worship of Zeus. The tradition is, although it isn't actually reported in the Maccabees, that a one day supply of consecrated oil miraculously lasted eight days. Today, lighting a candle every day for eight days is the main part of the celebration.

It's fascinated me to muse that the reestablishment of the Jerusalem Temple and rekindling of its light is the main focus of Chanukkah ceremonies and not the actual warfare and military victory of Judas Maccabee.

Liberation of Judea from Syrian oppression in the second century before Jesus is important to his present day followers because if Antiochus had successfully quashed Judaism, Jewish culture, Jewish traditions, and Jewish practices, Jesus would have been quite different, if there had been a Jesus at all.

From the importance of his coming "from the house and line" of King David (Matthew 1:20; Luke 2:4), through his circumcision in the rededicated Temple on the eighth day (Luke 2:2:21-22) and his interpretations of Hebrew law, to his symbolic fulfillment of the Jewish sacrificial system (John 1:29; Hebrews *passim*), Jesus can be understood only in the Jewish milieu which, thanks to the Maccabees, survived in spite of Antiochus' intention to extirpate and annihilate it.

Apart from all the theological justification, Chanukah is a fun time! In the home every evening for eight days a candle is lit in the menorah, the eight branched candle stick. Eight! Double the paltry practice in many Christian congregations of lighting four candles, one new one on each of the four Sundays before Christmas.

Eight candles instead of four! I've often wanted to suggest to congregations I served that they double the four candles in their Advent wreaths and after they light one candle in the pair to anticipate Jesus' birth they could light the second candle of the pair and give thanks for the survival of Jesus' people amid Syrian attempts to eradicate their culture. Christianity's Jewish heritage deserves acknowledgement and celebration!

I never made the suggestion; usually I'd already made enough strange suggestions and I'm well aware this one is strange. But I do think there should be some formal affirmation of our shared heritage.

Nonetheless, even without formal acknowledgement and celebration, Jesus' current followers should at the very least thank their Jewish neighbors for being the part of the seedbed out of which Jesus grew and in which he functioned. And also wish them a resoundingly Happy Hann . . . Chann . . . Hanu . . . a brilliantly Festive Festival of lights! (Wishes for seasonal *shalom* can be sent to: bohmhome@shentel.net)

- - - - -

A newspaper headline reported Pat Robertson's claim that God smote Ariel Sharon. My response resumed the theme of how the Bible is properly used.

- - - - -

Smote Signals
NVD January 7, 2006

God smote Ariel Sharon, Israel's Prime Minister, claimed Pat Robertson.

Maybe God did; maybe God didn't. I'm not sure how to evaluate Robertson's claim. And I don't take every statement I read on faith, Lutheran clergyperson though I may be.

Unlike the Bishop of Rome, the Bishop of Broadcasting lacks the mantle of infallibility. And even papal infallibility is active only under carefully prescribed circumstances. I can't imagine them being used to accuse the Maker of ordering a hit on Israel's Prime Minister.

Robertson's claim can't be accepted as infallible and must be evaluated on some other basis than his credibility as a leading spokesperson for one segment of Christian people.

Would God do such a thing as smite Sharon? Of course! God smote all kinds of people: the firstborn of the oppressors in Egypt (Exodus 12:29), the complaining Israelites in the wilderness (Numbers 11:33), the inhabitants of the transporting area

(Numbers 32:4), the Gibeonites (Joshua 10:10), and the tribe of Benjamin (Judges 20:35).

(Actually it's only the King James translation that uses that wonderful word "smote," with its smearing, smudgy, smashing SM, its long and mournful O and its abrupt final, explosive T. The Revised Standard Version uses "struck," much less satisfying with its dull U and gutturally swallowed CK.)

Robertson is right to claim that God smites. But the question remains, is he right to claim that God smote Sharon? That's much harder to determine.

Meaning no disrespect and hoping no one reports me to my bishop, I'm afraid God is not very consistent with the divine smiting. Consider, for example, the case of King David. He was smitten by Bathsheba, had an illicit relationship with her, and contrived to have her husband killed. But he was not smitten by God as a result. One wonders how the current Prime Minister of modern Israel was more deserving of the smite than the King of ancient Israel. Favoritism because Jesus was going to be born "of the house and lineage of David"? I hope not!

Sharon's sin, according to Robertson, was his willingness to divide God's land of Israel. And yet God's land had been seriously divided after King Solomon into a northern kingdom, Israel, and a southern kingdom, Judah. The divine Majesty both allowed that particular division and treated no one smitefully.

Perhaps if we can determine that Sharon's sin was in fact exceptionally heinous we can consequently accept Robertson's claim that God smote him for it.

Robertson cited Joel as proof that dividing God's land is more apt to rouse the Creator's righteous rage than are adultery and murder, or the division of Solomon's kingdom. Actually the proof text in Joel is hard to find because Joel is only three chapters long and buried in the back of the Hebrew Bible among the minor prophets. Not an obvious example of causes for God's displeasure. But Robertson's school of thought about the Bible is that every verse is as important as every other and that four verses of begats are worth as much as four verses reporting Jesus' resurrection.

Joel 3:2 does report the Lord as announcing with displeasure that foreigners "have divided my land, cast lots for my people, traded boys for prostitute, and sold girls for wine." So Robertson is in a sense right:

God expresses dissatisfaction with the rending of his kingdom, but the rending is accomplished by foreigners and accompanied by traffic in children. Perhaps Robertson knows something about Sharon that hasn't leaked to the media!

Anyone foolish enough to play the game of taking one verse out of context and using it to prove a point can counter Robertson by choosing Exodus 22:21, or any of its abundant parallels such as Exodus 23:9, Leviticus 19:34!, Deuteronomy 10:19.

In these passages God advises – or, rather, lays down the law for the people in Israel: "You shall get along with a resident alien." The legitimate question arising from these texts is "How can Israelis and Palestinians get along together?" One answer might be – Sharon apparently thought so – "By the Israelis ceding some of their land for use by the resident aliens."

As usual with Scripture, text can be cited against text and the whole series of readings announcing that the land is given to the offspring of Abraham and Sarah is balanced by a whole series of encouragements that they be kind and generous in sharing with others what the Lord God first gave to them, whether the law or the land.

And while the debate continues, many of us in the Christian community need to assure our Jewish friends and neighbors that although he may speak for God, Pat Robertson does not speak for us.
(bohmhome@shentel.net)

- - - - -

The Week of Prayer for Christian Unity had rolled around again.

- - - - -

Christian Friendly Fire
NVD January 18, 2006

"Friendly" fire wreaks havoc not just on the battlefield but in the church as well. Verbal potshots loosely aimed or shotgun blasts scattered broadside by one community that bears Christ's name can unintentionally do serious damage to other communities that bear the same name. But it is much worse when the intention by one branch of Jesus' followers actually is to attack and hurt those in another branch.

Imagine an army trying both to protect its citadel from siege and at the same time to make advances on the enemy. But then those guarding from the walls begin to lob rocks and shoot not just at the hostile siegers but on those from their own army who, in a different company or platoon, have sallied forth at great risk to pursue the enemy over the hill. The platoon entrusted with defense of the front gates is randomly sniped at by the high command as they plot strategy up in the tower. The brigade that has fled a fierce encounter outside and is seeking safe readmittance at the back gates is barred and repulsed by the contingent on duty there. Hardly a sane and sensible way to wage a war.

At some times, and in some quarters still, that was in fact the situation among the different churches. All confessed the same faith, often in the same words using the Apostles or Nicene creed, but all nonetheless viciously criticized, attacked, and stabbed one another.

Worst were the horrors visited by Christians on the Jews, the same people of God from whom Jesus and his followers first arose and in whose covenant, according to Saint Paul, and with whose traditions the Church still stands.

Second, Protestants and Roman Catholics used to be especially hostile, from verbal attacks through throwing rocks at one another in the streets to the kind of internecine warfare that has plagued Ireland.

Then, among the divisions on the Protestant side of the army, denominations battled over infant baptism or believer baptism, episcopal authority or presbyterian governance, raising hands for praise or making the sign of the cross for blessing, the amount of honor appropriate for the virgin Mary, coming forward to share bread and wine or having it passed out in the pews, acknowledging and reinforcing couples in committed relationships of faithfulness or consigning them to hell, taking the Bible literally in every regard, especially the creation stories, or accepting that the Bible at times uses parable, folktale, legend, and poetic license as well as straightforward historicity, obeying the commandment to worship on the seventh day of the week, Saturday, or changing the commandment and worshipping on Sunday, the first day of the week.

And so on. I've even heard Orthodox Christians and Roman Catholic Christians argue vehemently about the proper way to make the sign of the cross, right to left or left to right, and condemn each other for doing it wrong.. I'm not sure if God laughs or cries. Probably both.

Outsiders praised the early followers of Jesus with the compliment "Behold how they love one another!" More recently the appropriate comment might have become "Behold how they love to quibble with one another."

Fortunately the tide has begun to turn and most Christian communities will be celebrating a week of prayer for Christian Unity extending from January 18, the day commemorating Peter's acknowledgement of Jesus as the Messiah, and January 25, when in a vision God called Saul of Tarsus, later known as St. Paul, to extend the covenant with Abraham and Sarah to the gentiles.

Denominations or congregations not convinced that they have a monopoly on the divine truth usually use this week to join in Jesus' prayer that his followers might be one. (John 17: 11,21-23) And in spite of the differences across denominational lines and sometimes even non-denominational lines there is cooperation on the church's, I mean the churches' mission to feed the hungry, care for the sick, encourage the downhearted, clothe the naked, and provide for the homeless.

"Onward, Christian soldiers, marching as to war," but for Heaven's sake not for war on one another but for war with one another against a common foe. Close ranks to fight injustice and poverty, meaninglessness and despair. If, instead of fighting side by side supportively with one another against the forces of darkness and evil, the loyal legions of the Lord fire on one another as if they were enemies, surely the real Enemy laughs. (respond to: bohmhome@shentel.net)

- - - - -

The religious writers of letters to the editor had been active again with attacks on secular humanists which I considered unfair and overdone, so I came to their defense with this editorial. As a result I was invited to be the speaker at one of the meetings of SASH, the Shenandoah Area Secular Humanists. I gladly accepted and a report of that meeting is the subject of a later editorial. Don't tell my bishop!

- - - - -

Secular Humanists
NVD January 26, 2006

"Secular Humanist" is a term that at least rouses hostile suspicions if not strikes terror in the hearts of some Christians. Hearing it, they would make the sign of the cross to avert the power of Satan and evil – if they were the kinds of Christians that make the sign of the cross.

I don't understand the negative reaction, Christian clergyperson though I am. Secular humanists believe in using reason and scientific methodology, without any need of divine revelation, to solve problems and provide standards for human conduct and interrelatedness. Naturally I'm hurt that they think that Someone I consider very important doesn't even exist, but hey! If that Someone can handle it, so can I.

The Creator of all certainly wants to be acknowledged, rightly, as the center of cosmic attention and must miss acknowledgment by secular humanists. But I am sure that the Creator of all not only endorses the secular humanist goals of solving world problems and working for harmony, peace, and sharing, but also roots for them as being on the same side and team. I'm just as sure the Creator of all gets very upset with those who claim to be on the divine side and team but undermine the divine plan by narrow clannishness and putting their own selfish interests ahead of the common good, the well being of the whole human race.

"Humanist" should be no problem. Although it used to mean scholars who read pagan poets like Vergil because of their interest in humanity in all its variety, not just Christian, it has come to mean being interested in or committed to humanity, being humane, having humanitarian intentions. Who would object to a group that wants to be known as humane? (We shan't digress here into whether or not it's proper to name an Animal Interest Group a "Humane" Society, as if animals have the same status as humans. Maybe on another occasion.)

"Secular," is from a Latin word that even appears on our dollar bills with "In God we trust" in the form *saeculorum*, in the phrase from the Roman poet Virgil: *Nova ordo saeculorum,* "new order of the world" or "new world order." Given the way the world's been going for the past four thousand years, I'm all in favor of a new order of things! America's founding fathers, who read Virgil, and probably also our founding mothers, who did not, were hoping for a nation where liberty and justice for all would usher in the kind of golden age also described by the pagan poet Virgil. Boy, were they mistaken! Ask, among others, any black person.

"Secular" means simply "worldly," but unfortunately often has a negative sense of being too interested in or dedicated to worldly goodies. Christians have been reminded by their chief rabbi that they are indeed "worldly'", that is "in the world," though they should not be "of the world" (John 17: 11, 16). We're worldly – in this world – just as our Leader was (John 3:17, never shown at football games) whether we like it or not. We can pretend to some kind of otherworldliness and withdraw into aloof indifference or narrow isolationism, or we can admit our involvement and mix it up with the mud, muck, and mire of this order of things, just as our Leader did. Maybe even relate not only with sinners and tax collectors but also with secular humanists in an effort to improve this temporary world at least temporarily and to foster understanding and good will.

I certainly would never give up on participating in weekly sharing of the Story and of the bread and wine in Jesus' name, but I wouldn't be completely uncomfortable attending gatherings of secular humanists to discuss how to protect our environment and increase fairness and cooperation, liberty and justice for all this quarrelsome race called human. I'd consider myself an undercover agent of the Divine, helping an organization which some of my fellow believers count as the enemy to work for goals of which the Creator resoundingly approves.

I'd just miss the fun of singing hymns or songs. (Send secular humanist meeting notices to bohmhome@shentel.net)

- - - - -

Headlines about the aftermath of the destruction caused by hurricane Katrina in the fall ranged from encomia of people who helped to denunciations of people who hindered. My musings in this editorial stray from my normal theme of Biblical interpretation into theology.

- - - - -

Good and Bad
NVD February 8, 2006

Katrina renewed attention to an old question about human nature: are people basically good or basically bad?

Looting and plundering, compounded by dereliction of duty and violation of solemn oaths of service by members of the New Orleans Police Department are cited as factual evidence for the fictional view in Golding's *Lord of the Flies*: deep down under the shallow veneer of civilized goodness people are vicious, savage, and selfish. We're bad!

Outpourings of financial assistance and altruistic sacrifice of time to slosh through mud, slime, and sewage overflows, on the other hand, were cited by more than one journalist covering the hurricane as evidence that when the chips are down and the flood waters up people are basically sympathetic, caring, and selfless. We're good!

Christian clergy-person though I am, I never understood the question of whether humanity, and by implication I myself, belong in a box labeled "good" or "bad." True, one of our former worship books had me confessing every Sunday that "we are by nature sinful and unclean." And I certainly had enough experience to understand and accept the "sinful and unclean" part. But "by nature" puzzled me and does still.

Scripture says very little about "nature" or the "natural;" check your concordance or theological word books. The Bible doesn't deal with those metaphysical questions so dear to Greek philosophers: "What Is it?' "What is its Nature?" "Is it true to its Nature?" Scripture describes rather than defines. Only a few later Biblical writers, primarily Paul, begin tentatively to introduce language about human "nature."

Building on Paul, Augustine, the late fourth century North African theological marvel, both blended and redirected Greek and Biblical views for all subsequent Christian thought. Greek philosophers like Plato and Aristotle had written about "natures" and had a positive view of human nature, assuming if people knew what was right or good, they'd do it. Biblical writers tended to avoid talking about human "nature" and had a rather pessimistic view of humanity: if it was possible to misbehave, people would.

Augustine made the pessimistic view the normative category for human nature. We don't just commit sins, we are "by nature" sinful and unclean. We are all flawed and broken, and apart from God's grace patching and mending us, we cannot be good no matter how many good things we manage to do.

Are table knives good or bad? They are designed to cut or to spread, not to shovel peas into one's mouth or catapult mashed potato gobs across a dining hall for a food fight. In terms of their design they're good for some activities, bad for others. In terms of actual function apart from design or intent, most knives I've known are better as catapults than as cutters, especially of the kind of meat served at summer camp.

Saint Augustine would claim by analogy that all human beings are like broken table knives. Our "nature" is incomplete. We might be able to do good things, as the table knife can spread butter, or bad things, as the table knife can lob gobs, but we are basically "bad" because we are not fully what we were designed and intended to be.

Are people basically good or bad? As with the table knife, the answer depends in part on the purpose of humanity, for which different schools of thought would give very different answers.

Don't tell my bishop: I have serious trouble with this concept of "original sin" and "by nature sinful." When I look into my own heart I do indeed find a deep tendency and drive always to put myself first and be in control and I know it's inevitable that I yield to that tendency and drive. I hope I wouldn't have been a plundering policeman in New Orleans, but I understand those who were.

Simultaneously I find in myself an equally natural, deep tendency and drive to help, to care, to sacrifice for someone else, even for strangers. There is a counter movement within my will that goes in the opposite direction from selfishness. I give to help Katrina victims and I feel the impulse that led some people to travel to New Orleans.

Good and bad impulses within me I understand. They're both part of my human experience. But "by nature bad" – or good – I do not understand.

To identify general categories like human beings as basically, by nature, 'good' or 'bad' is probably a mistake. It is more helpful to avoid thus classifying political parties, and Protestants or Roman Catholics, and atheists or theists. It's natural, of course, to put labels on. But it might be a really bad idea.
(bohmhome@shentel.net)

- - - - -

After that digression into theology or philosophy, here I am back into Bible study for the next two editorials. The first repeats material from the Noah's ark series that I forget I had written about environmental guidelines but does include new reflections on the use of drugs.

- - - - -

Finding Relevant Commandments
NVD February 13, 2006

Finding suitable guidelines in the Bible for some aspects of twenty-first century life can be difficult.

"Thou shalt do no drugs" appears nowhere among all the commandments because use of drugs was not an issue in scriptural times. We can, of course, by extension apply statements about the Biblical drug of choice, alcohol, to the wide variety of drugs in use today, marijuana, cocaine, meth, LSD, or whatever. But if we do that, we wind up with an interesting situation and a probably unpopular conclusion.

Although there are no laws against alcohol among the 613 rabbinic commandments in the Torah, two interesting and possibly relevant statements are made about wine in less significant Old Testament books: "Wine is a deceiver... Whoever is led astray by it is not wise," warns Proverbs 20:1 On the other hand, "God created plants... to bring forth... wine to gladden the human heart," celebrates Psalm 104:15 with a parallel in Ecclesiastes 10:19. Neither is a "Thou shalt" or "Thou shalt not" statement, but it might be inferred that wine dare be used for gladdening, but not used to the extent that it deceives and leads astray.

Since the Bible does not prohibit alcohol but rather seems to allow its use cautiously and moderately, can we conclude that other drugs are not prohibited but allowed if used cautiously and moderately?

Paul encourages Timothy "Take a little wine for your stomach's sake and your frequent ailments." (1 Timothy 5:23) Might he similarly have suggested "Smoke a little pot to help relieve your stress" if the fruit of the cannabis was as commonly available then as the fruit of the vine? Or since the effects of today's drugs are much more powerful than the effects of naturally fermented wine, unfortified or distilled, in Bible times, is it unfair to draw the parallel?

"Thou shalt not kill" has been applied, with extensive press coverage, to the withdrawal of life support systems. Even back then there were obviously exceptions: people killed others in times of war with impunity and in one mind-boggling story Jephtha cold-bloodedly kills his own daughter without reproach or repercussions. (Judges 11:30-31, 39) Today, could withdrawal of a respirator, a possibility totally unknown when the commandments touched down on Sinai, similarly be another acceptable exception?

Environmental guidelines are easier to find in Scripture, not in the writings of Jesus' followers because they all believed the existing scheme of things was going to end within their lifetime. (1 Thessalonians 4:15; 1 Peter 4:7; Mark 19:1) Why take good care of the earth when before too long there would be a new heaven and a new earth? (Revelation 21:1)

"Thou shalt not pollute thy lakes" or "Thou shalt preserve species" cannot be found. But a sense of responsibility for the created realm occurs already in Genesis' first chapter when the Creator passes to humanity control over all that has been created, presumably to maintain by good stewardship, not to misuse by plundering and destroying.

More explicitly a relevant commandment is given in Deuteronomy 22:6-7: if you come upon a bird's nest with eggs or fledglings, you dare take the eggs and fledglings but "You shall not take the mother. Let the mother go." Extrapolating, we have an excellent middle ground between the two extremes of "Wipe them all out" and "Don't touch them at all." Presumably the mother is saved as more likely to survive than the eggs or little ones and thus better able to continue the species. Principles of moderation and concern for future generations radiate from this little commandment.

From this should probably not be extrapolated a divine sanction for "survival of the fittest."

Balance, proportion, harmony, and moderation as environmental principles radiate also from Psalm 104, describing God as creating various foods, various regions, and various times for various creatures: grass for cattle, plants for people; trees for birds, mountains for goats, rocky places for rodents; night time for forest animals to prowl, daytime for people to labor. This description, neither thorough nor accurate, breathes a sense of balance, of interrelatedness and mutual dependence, that would be appreciated by any environmentalist, even one who didn't believe God had a hand in the setup.

God has not provided in one special book a complete set of written laws that cover thoroughly and in detail, without any need for interpretation, all modern contingencies like drug use, life support systems, and environmental concerns. Nonetheless, although some may doubt the divine Wisdom for doing so, human nature being what it is, the Creator, it seems, trusts human intelligence accurately to extrapolate and interpret from the laws that have already been given relevant laws for the contemporary world.

- - - - -

Snow Job
NVD February 11, 2006

I don't like snow. Some people do, I know, and they're welcome to it. They can also help themselves any time to the snow that accumulates on my deck, walkway, and drive. It's theirs free for the carting away.

As a serious, biblically oriented Christian clergy-person, I muse about the meaning of snow in the Bible What do the Holy Scriptures say about those tiny, frozen, delicate, six pointed water crystals, each unique, that look so seductively beautiful drifting lazily down out of the sky but then become such a heavy, burdensome nuisance as they deepen, drift, block highways, and strain backs?

Not too much. Perhaps Scripture follows the old adage – well, new adage compared to the age of Scripture itself – "If you can't say something nice, don't say anything at all."

Most of the very few biblical references to snow, according to my concordances, are to its bright whiteness, including the only three mentions in the Christian section of the Good Book: Jesus' cloak at the transfiguration (Mark 9:3), the angel at the tomb (Matthew 28:3), and the beard of the Enthroned Majesty (Revelation 1:14). Job 37:5 cites snow as the first example after claiming "God does great things we cannot comprehend." Can't comprehend why God made snow? Amen to that!

All our normal associations with snow – snowmen, I mean snowpeople, sledding, sleighing, and snowball fights – are obviously unmentioned in a book written in an area where snow was rare and unusual.

Scripture was naturally limited to a large extent by the location and culture of those who wrote it. It has, for example, not only just scanty references to snow, but, alas, no references at all to beer, though the Egyptians right next door to Israel had been quaffing fermented grain, one assumes happily, since before Abram and Sarai left Ur of the Chaldeans. Does lack of mention mean disapproval? Was the Divine Eye looking the other way? Or was it simply that Biblical writers were unfamiliar with what many consider one of God's good gifts?

Unmentioned also are volcanoes and vodka, hurricanes and hammocks, glaciers and glockenspiels, none of which was part of life and experience in the Holy Land.

Besides omissions like these, the Bible sometimes takes an unusual slant on something familiar, like the sea.

Hebrew folk in Bible times were landlubbers who hated the sea, which for them meant the Mediterranean, that amorphous and seething mass of water extending beyond sight and beyond thought, on which only crazy goyim like the Philistines would dare to sail. Galilee, mentioned often, wasn't like the real "sea," it was just a lake on which travelers never need fear being out of sight of land.

Primal chaos was represented to them by the vast expanses of water whose division into waters above and waters below was God's first task in creation after turning on the lights. (Genesis 1:1-3) And of course the story of the destructive flood – sea everywhere! – was both fed by and also fed into Hebrew oceanic anxieties.

Addressing that pervasive cultural phenomenon of Hebrew dislike and fear of the sea, Revelation 21:1 offers the reassurance that in the world to come "The Sea will be no more."

Early believers, coming out of a Jewish background, would have heard that news with great relief. But how that news, taken literally, can upset the host of modern believers who are foolish enough to enjoy getting sand in their bathing suits and salt water in their eyes while running the risk of jelly-fish and perhaps even sharks. I've seen adults weep nonetheless at the prophesied prospect of no more sea for all eternity.

I try to reassure them that perhaps the passage isn't literally true but culturally determined, that it speaks both out of and to the Hebrew fear of the sea, that it's really saying "causes of fear" will be no more. Wiping tears from their eyes, they respond, "But it's in the **Bible**!"

I've learned it doesn't pay to argue with that, so all I do is try to get through to them subliminally by whistling the Gershwin tune: "It ain't necessarily so . . . the things that you're liable to read in the Bible."

And while I whistle I hope there'll be no snow in the world to come either.

(Snow removal volunteers: bohmhome@shentel.net)

- - - - -

I'd had favorable personal responses by e-mail to a number of my editorials; "Snow Job" earned me a personal response which, in addition to heatedly criticizing my style of Biblical interpretation, picked up on my reference to Gerschwin and advised me "You're not likely to be singing "'swonderful'" where you'll be going, Reverend." A delightful reply to my own use of Gerschwin!

Back to the conflict between the atheists and the religious community . . .

- - - - -

Imagine It
NVD February 6, 2006

"I simply cannot imagine what it would be like to believe in God," says the atheist.

"I just can't imagine how someone can't believe in God," says the Christian.

That's one of the major problems with this world – too many people are too thoroughly lacking in imagination! Locked in their own small thought worlds, they're reluctant to open the door, step out, and peep at an alternate possibility.

Imagination unfortunately tends to have bad publicity. The phrase "It's just your imagination" means "Don't take it seriously" or "It doesn't really count" and the word "imaginary" has overtones or undercurrents of unreality. A child's imaginary friend isn't really there.

Thus are the products of "imagination" dismissed in the practical world.

In the impractical world of art, cinema, theater, and literature, however, imagination does have a positive value. "An imaginative work of fiction" or "a painting which shows imaginativeness" are both terms of appreciation and approval. We expect to suspend our disbelief when we enter into the imaginary world of a play or movie, but then the curtain falls or the house lights come on and it's back to "reality."

Imagination, for all the fun, amusement, and entertainment it can provide, sometimes seems antithetical to the real, the practical, and the serious.

Without imagination, however, the real and practical and serious areas of science and technology would not have made their advances.

Could you imagine a way to measure the distance from the Earth to the Sun? Hipparchus could. In the second century before the birth of Jesus he had two simultaneous sightings taken of the Sun's angle from two locations far distant from one another. With those angles and that distance he was able to calculate the distance rather accurately. He just had to exercise his imagination.

Distances to stars in our galaxy? Could you imagine? Of course! Just use as a baseline between the sighted angles to a star the distance that separates Earth's orbital positions at a sixth month interval. And from our galaxy to other galaxies, where the angles are too infinitivally small to measure for trigonometric calculations? Ingeniously using the cycles and comparative brightnesses of stars whose magnitudes fluctuate, imaginative astronomers are able to calculate the distances even to the galaxies.

Imagination opens a door into a strange landscape where things are other than what we're used to. Imagine there's a large, strange creature at the top of a beanstalk that has grown up into the clouds. Imagine how much light could be generated if an electrical current is passed though a thin enough conductor. Imagine the conflict that would arise when a boy and girl from feuding families fall in love. Imagine generating enough wind with a motor driven propeller to lift an extended set of wings. Imagine how to harness a head of steam or the explosion of gas and use it to drive pistons and thus to power . . . let's see, what all could we power?

Radio and television, cell phones and computers, gasoline engines and earth orbiting satellites, lasers and cyclotrons, x-rays and electrocardiograms, open heart surgery and DNA splicing – all are the final products in the real world of something that began just in someone's imagination.

Imagination is a very important part of humanity's mental make-up, but can imagination be taught? Probably not the extent of imagination used and enjoyed by Sophocles or Einstein, by Shakespeare or Edison. But yes, we do speak of "exercising" our imaginations. Imagination comes naturally; consider how imaginative a child can be without any training. Children's imaginations need pruning; further along the age line, however, imagination may need cultivation.

One way we cultivate it is by involvement in the worlds of art. Another way we cultivate it is by involvement in conversation with someone whose take on reality is radically different from our own. The atheists works at imagining how the Christian views the world; the Christian imagines how an atheist can live contently and even happily and morally in a world without a God. Both grow as a result of their imaginative exercise.

Perhaps if the European newspapers had paused to imagine what would be the likely results in the Arab communities of their Muhammad cartoons they wouldn't have precipitated the crisis; perhaps if Muslims could have imagined the mindset and presuppositions of the Danish news they would not have turned so violent.

Imagination can be the foundation of a new reality. Just imagine it! (Imaginative responses are welcome at: bohmhome@shentel.net)

- - - - -

"Imagine it" also earned me a personal response from a person who very radically misinterpreted what I thought I was saying. He thought I was saying if you could imagine it then it was real. Wouldn't it be nice! My point was that something like belief in God or disbelief in God, a poem by A. E. Housman or an ode by Keats or world peace or the reconciliation of opposing groups cannot become real without first being pictured or imagined.

After that editorial attempt at getting atheists and theists to use their imaginations to try to think sympathetically about one another, I finally fulfilled my speaking engagement with SASH, the Shenandoah Area Secular Humanists, as reported below. The original title was "Daniel, no lyin'." The NVD's substitution works much better.

- - - - -

In the Humanists' Den
NVD March 8, 2006

"Daniel in the lions' den" was the prediction of my friends and clergy colleagues for my appearance as an invited guest speaker among the atheists who meet with the Shenandoah Area Secular Humanists on February 18.

I could understand what aroused their fears. From a member of that group had frequently come rather harsh and virulent letters to this newspaper's editor militantly attacking religion and practitioners of religion. And there I would be, not only a practitioner, but one who taught others to be practitioners.

Letters also accused religions of being, in effect, the Mothers of All Evils. Letters implied that anyone in this post-enlightenment world who still believed in God or the supernatural was crazy or stupid or both.

One clergy colleague reminded me of those letters. I told him that I figured if the whole group thought I were crazy or stupid, they wouldn't have wanted to listen to me.

"Daniel in the lions' den," he responded. "They don't want to listen to you. They want to devour you."

Personal presence and a group, in my experience, usually makes communication easier and expressions of hostility more difficult. The kind of sniping and name calling that is easy in a Letter to the Editor becomes more difficult in a face to face encounter when there are other people around who may not be so harsh and virulent and who may resent someone who is.

Perhaps, I mused aloud after sharing that opinion with my colleagues, that's one of the meanings in the Christian doctrine – or myth, or symbolic statement – that God became a personal, flesh and blood presence in Jesus of Nazareth. God could literally rub elbows and break bread and talk and listen and respond. Up close and personal works better, I claimed.

"Didn't he wind up," someone interjected, "on a cross?"

My announced topic was "Christians and Humanists: Can We Talk?" Obviously I thought we could in spite of the major difference or I wouldn't have accepted their invitation.

And talk we did. Comfortably and congenially. It was wonderful.

We talked about the difficulty of dialogue. The more deeply held our convictions the more difficult dialogue is. We feel threatened when our strongest beliefs are not accepted by the other side; we want the affirmation provided by the other side coming to agree with our view. We would rather convert than understand. But it spite of the admitted difficulties we were able to dialogue smoothly.

We talked about a recent Northern Virginia Daily article about scientific research on people with deeply held political opinions. Brain scans indicated that the reasoning sections of their minds disengaged when information challenged those opinions and that their mental reactions became emotional rather than rational. For some people under some circumstances, it seems, rational discourse is – alas – not possible.

We talked about what is meant by "Christians" and "Humanists." Dialogue can be impeded by an erroneous caricature of the dialogue partner. Some humanists hear the name "Christian" and picture rigid, evangelical fanatics or think of the priest who got too cozy with them in the sacristy when they were altar boys. Some Christians hear the name "humanists" and think "atheists" and picture immoral hedonists who immorally pursue their own pleasures without any concept of right or wrong or fear of punishment.

We talked also of Christians who can listen patiently to those with a very different world view. We talked about people who do not believe in God and yet do not put their own selfish purposes first but are committed with diligence and even self-sacrifice to working for the common good, for helping the poor, caring for the needy, striving for mutual understanding and reconciliation, protecting the environment, and in general prospering the condition of humanity on the planet we all share.

We avoided our major difference, the God question, and we reflected that agreeing on a topic and sticking to it is very important. There's no real communication if the Christians want to talk about how to feed the local hungry and the atheists keep asking them "Why are you so stupid as to believe in God?" Conversely, conversation goes nowhere if the atheists are trying to talk about local environmental issues and the Christians just keep urging them to give their hearts to the Lord Jesus.

Most important, we talked. I'm going to encourage my skeptical friends and colleagues that they find opportunities to do the same. (Dialogue through bohmhome@shentel.net)

- - - - -

For the most part my editorials try to respect the differences between atheists and the religious and are more concerned about encouraging them to get along in spite of their differences than to win anyone over. But I started musing about conversion and wound up writing . . .

- - - - -

Religious Convertibles
NVD March 11, 2006

Religions are a combination of threat and promise for outsiders planning to convert from no religion or from one to another.

Consider the threats. If I were to convert to Judaism, not only would I incur the wrath of my Lutheran bishop, I would be expected to give up lobster and shrimp, pork and bacon. A potential convert to Islam faces similar threats – well, maybe not a bishop's wrath – as well as giving up alcohol and Friday as a work day. Women converts will lose the chance to show off their features.

Some Christian denominations insist on a pledge of tithing before accepting a new member. Becoming a Roman Catholic means believing that in certain circumstances a papal pronouncement is as infallible as fundamentalists insist the Bible is. And Lutherans are expected to strain their voices at least four times a year on the high notes of "A Mighty Fortress."

All of the varied groups claiming to follow Jesus threaten converts with major changes in their lifestyles. They will be expected not just to fight their natural urge to be vindictive and retaliatory but even to attempt to love their enemies and pray for them. They will be expected to wrestle against greed and gluttony. They will be expected to help strangers and care for the poor and needy, the homeless and outcasts.

Of course in all religious systems the threat is offset by a promise or expectation. Were I to decide to give up seafood and pig meat and be grafted into Judaism I would have the blessed assurance of being part of the eternal covenant God made with Abraham and Sarah four thousand years ago. Any covenant strong enough to last that long in spite of the hatred shown by Pharaoh's armies and Roman legions, in the pograms and the Holocaust, must have something going for it!

Converts to Christianity have the promise that they'll stroll streets of gold in the afterlife. (Revelation 21:21) I'm not sure that's worth living up to some of the difficult here-and-now expectations, but then too there is the promise of existence without tears or pain, without sorrow or crying. (Revelation 21:4) There is the promise of "the healing of the nations." (Revelation 22: 2) Haste the day!

Not just otherworldly promises and rewards offset the threats and difficulties of making a commitment to a religious community. Sometimes here-and-now benefits are offered. Having faced the threats and accepted the difficulties involved in life after conversion, the convert will gain something. Good, extensive new business contacts! Social acceptability! Community prestige!

Apart from those benefits, of dubious value, religious communities offer indeed the promise of camaraderie and celebration, of a sense of cosmic meaning and direction for life. Whether the offers are fulfilled, and fulfilling, or not, it might be worth a preliminary try.

Balance the expectations – "what must I do?" – against the rewards – "what will I get out of it? Will it be worth it?"

Whoa! "What will I get out of it?" Is that indeed the right question? Certainly it has grown over recent decades to become one of today's major motivational questions. But there's a fairer, more primal question. Is it true?

Is it true that the Creator of all things is bound to the offspring of Abraham and Sarah by an eternal commitment? Is it true that the Lord of the universe was at work in a special and unique way in Jesus of Nazareth, reclaiming a humanity that had forgotten its true purpose? Is it true that the Divine One designated Muhammad the last prophet or that the angel Mormon directed Joseph Smith to tablets written with a special revelation?

Long time atheist C. S. Lewis, whose "The Lion, the Witch, and the Wardrobe," recently was made into a movie, reports about his conversion in his autobiography, *Surprised by Joy*: "In 1929 I gave in . . . and prayed: perhaps, that night, the most dejected and reluctant convert in all England." He had been won over in spite of his stubborn resistance not by any happy hope of gain but by the simple conviction that the Christian message was true.

For potential converts to any religion the basic question should not be the one so popular in the first decade of this new millennium: "What's in it for me?" Rather it should be the question with much more eternal resonance: "Is it true?" (Responses are welcome: bohmhome@shentel.net)

- - - - -

In spite of weekly sermons, regular adult classes, and midweek discussions of the Bible, many people in congregations I've served have acquired from popular culture some strange ideas about our faith. Some of those sources are tabloid newspapers . . .

- - - - -

Tabloid Theology
NVD March 23, 2006

People reading this excellent newspaper presumably have too much sense to read the tabloids. Normally I avoid them too, but I was stuck in the barber shop and the headline of the tabloid on the table had a religious flair, so, being a clergyman, I picked it up and read it.

Reports on the front page – details inside – announced that Jesus was soon coming. That certainly cheered me up. Heaven knows this world needs all the outside help it can get. Jesus. Elijah. Whoever.

I turned to the inside pages for the further reassurance that couldn't have been read in the tabloid cover by someone standing in a supermarket line who would have had to buy a copy.

What a disappointment! The authority for the article's sure and certain announcement of the Galilean rabbi's imminent reappearance had been five "theologians" I had never heard of. A graduate of Princeton Seminary and Union Seminary and former faculty member at New York Theological Seminary, I'm no stranger to a wide variety of religious circles.

Consequently I didn't take their alleged authorities for the news of Jesus' prompt return too seriously. But if their prediction turns out to be wrong they'll be in very good company. Even that very respected theologian, St. Paul, erroneously announced that Jesus would return while he was still alive (1 Thessalonians 4:5). And, of all people, he was wrong. So I won't be hard on five unknown theologians if they too happen to be wrong.

Always interested, however, in giving a fair hearing, I did read further to find out what other justification there might be for keeping alive hopes that the risen one will return to make all things new before our next national elections. Further evidence in the article cited to prove Jesus would be back soon was an interpretation of a quote from the Dead Sea scrolls. Whenever you want to give extra oomph to a tabloid article, or an academic paper for that matter, quote the Dead Sea scrolls.

I've worked in the Dead Sea Scrolls enough to know that none of them has a reference to Jesus by name. Some scrolls do speak about a "righteous leader," but that's a generic title and may or may not refer to the man from Nazareth. Amid the turmoil, confusion, and upheaval in first century Judea there was naturally a great deal of hope for any "righteous leader" who could set things straight, whether divine or human or something in between. But the article claimed the scrolls said something about Jesus specifically, making a leap of faith I'd hesitate to make, especially since the Dead Sea scroll it was referring to was not a biblical book.

Aramaic, the tabloid also explained, had been the language of the Hebrew Bible or, as the tabloid put it, the "Old Testament." Of a few later books, yes, but the tabloid was quoting Genesis, which is very definitely in Hebrew. That was the point at which I stopped reading and gave up the optimistic anticipation that this sorry scheme of things would soon give way to a kingdom of justice and mercy in which the poor would not be at the mercy of the federal budget.

Tabloids with all this kind misinformation and distortions sell. They sell very well. In fact I've even thought of writing and selling them an article or two, but my academic integrity and the kind of articles they'd buy are in major, insurmountable conflict.

As a clergyman I'm ashamed to admit: It's to a great extent the churches' own fault that superficial and even erroneous religious articles help sell tabloids. Churches unfortunately have not often enough taught their people to deal critically with the Bible. I don't mean "critical" in the sense of being totally negative and reprimanding, but in the way a drama critic or literary critic works: Analyze and evaluate. Instead, the mantra "The Bible says . . ." or even "A Dead Sea scroll says . . ." becomes a protective mantle to prevent debate and discussion, evaluation and interpretation.

Thank goodness for the Northern Virginia Daily to counteract the tabloids.
(bohmhome@shentel.net)

- - - - -

In my work as an interim pastor serving congregations in a wide area of central and eastern Pennsylvania and northwestern Virginia I've subscribed to many newspapers and have discovered, as I say in the previous editorial, that among them all the *Northern Virginia Daily* is indeed a gem.

One of its strengths is its even-handedness, although conservatives sometimes accuse it of liberal bias if there's a political cartoon they don't like and liberals claim it tilts too far to the right if there's an editorial they dislike. Differing groups with differing perspectives – liberal and conservative, fundamentalist Christian and secular humanist, Presbyterians and Pentecostals – experience different "kinds of reality," as explored in the following item.

- - - - -

Many Kinds of 'Reality'
NVD March 25, 2006

"Reality" TV shows have me musing about the meaning of their generic title. Are they called 'reality' shows because they claim to be unscripted and spontaneous in contrast to 'unreality' shows that are planned and rehearsed in advance?

Or are the kinds of things those shows depict supposed to be aspects of the "real" world, such common and everyday activities as eating ugly bugs and worms, or risking life, limb, and sanity in preposterous predicaments, or engaging in fierce, cutthroat competition, all presented in an atmosphere of emotional intensity, high anxiety, and terror?

If the reason for the title is the former, the alleged unscripted spontaneity, I suspect some watchers nonetheless assume the reason is really the latter: that unusual circumstances involving preposterous tasks are in fact what "reality" means. Since their own everyday world is dull and uninteresting, bring on the tension and testing. That's the real thing that makes the juices flow and proves one is alive.

Probably I shouldn't even mention reality TV shows since I've never seen one, only their advertising come-ons. But then again, as a Christian clergyperson well trained at some excellent seminaries, I have extensive experience discussing, analyzing, and evaluating many things I have never really seen, like God, the Holy Spirit, angels, demonic powers, and the Church as a cooperative group of committed believers who put their energy into improving the world rather than bickering among themselves.

Justifiably or not, those shows which I have never seen have me musing about the meaning of "reality."

Scientists, especially physicists and chemists, in all probability and with a bit of uncertainty, would claim that everything is really a complex interplay of charged particles spinning one way or another but able to be represented also as waves even though there is no medium through which the waves roll.

Some of them even define ultimate reality by string theory. In weaker moments I suspect they're all willing parts of a complex conspiracy and chuckling at their awareness that they're really just stringing the rest of us along.

"Reality" for artists, who might find its interpretation by mathematical equations mechanical and tedious, means form and shape and size and colors and hues and tones.

"Reality" for the homeless, starving waif wandering back alleys of Calcutta will not mean the same thing that it does for the Oxford don who has finished his afternoon tutorial sessions and is heading to the pub for a pint.

Some have even claimed that our president is living in a very different reality, to which others have responded in exasperation, "Oh, really!"

Previous generations never raised questions about ultimate reality as critically as the question has been raised recently when particle accelerators enable us to see if a muon spins, and the world of the Oxford don is closer and more familiar with the world of the Calcutta waif. Moreover, the sixties mind-set of "different strokes for different folks" has also permeated American culture enough that people are more open to the possibility that one person's reality may be another's fantasy, and vice versa..

Ultimate reality means different things to different people; ultimately our view depends on our particular perspective and the place from which we're viewing.

Complicating this situation is the impossibility of proving what is "real." If my reality differs from yours but is the standard by which I judge what is real, how can I convince you, who have a different ultimate standard, that my reality is right or true and yours is not? Or vice versa. The measuring criteria each of us uses are incompatible and immutable.

Among multiple realities some people live in a reality without any divine Power; others inhabit a reality where a benevolent Power is ultimately in charge, in spite of horrors and nastiness along the way; yet others dwell in a reality whose ultimate Authority is the kind of warped and vindictive personality who would be good at dreaming up stunts for "reality" TV shows.

A corollary and a problem arise.

Corollary: we all need to be patient with those whose reality is radically different from our own. Try to visit the other world.

Get a feel for it. Try it on for size. Watch the reality TV show even if it's a different world.

Problem: how patient dare the person in a reality whose bedrock is kindness and fairness be with a person whose ultimate reality has self-gratification as its goal and unbridled violence as its means?

In this tension between patience and problem, we wait and work in hope that behind our separate realties there is in fact a true Ultimate Reality which breaks through and corrects or overcomes the false.

- - - - -

Although most of the following is fictional and no bishop ever challenged me about it, it is true that I once did three baptisms in a stream at Zion Stone Church, New Ringgold, Pennsylvania. Jestingly I had asked three teenagers preparing for baptism if they wanted to do it "Bible-style" – in the stream down the hill from the church. I should have known better than to jest! Seriously they responded, "Yes!" So that's the way we did it. Sunday evening many members of the congregation gathered to see what was not a normal practice for Lutherans. We sang a hymn, used the Apostles Creed as a confession of our faith, and everyone except the three candidates and their sponsors crossed the stream, appropriately named Jordan. The candidates each answered a form of the traditional questions, were baptized, and climbed the opposite bank to rejoin the others amid song, laughter, and embracing.

The offer in the last paragraph of this editorial is still good!

- - - - -

A Lutheran Baptist
NVD April 5, 2006

"Relocating to an area with a lot of Baptists might be a good idea for you," my northern bishop suggested. He had found out I had performed a baptism by total immersion. That's not the way our Lutheran denomination normally does it.

Normally I too perform a baptism by sloshing water, saying the candidate's name, and pronouncing the words, "I baptize you . . ." I've always felt rather dumb doing it that way because "baptize" is from a Greek word that means "dunk." So there I am in front of a congregation splashing water while saying to the splashee, in effect, "I dunk you," and hoping no one notices the discrepancy between my words and my deed. Heaven knows I give them enough other opportunities to notice that.

In spite of my denomination's rigid preference for sprinkling I had always wanted to try immersion. As I regularly point out to everyone requesting a baptism, going completely under the water and coming back out is the way it happened in the Bible and certainly fulfills the imagery of being "born again of water and the Spirit" (John 3:5) and "being buried together with Christ by baptism into death" (Romans 6:4).

Biblical reasons never seem to matter as much to baptismal candidates as other criteria. For parents it's safety: "You mean you'd put our little darling all the way under?" Teenagers or adults have yet other concerns: "What would I wear? How much would I have to take off? How cold is the water?"

Somewhere in the discussion they all take refuge behind an argument that's a guaranteed winner in church circles: "We've never done it that way before."

A public act of total commitment to one of the two sides in a cosmic conflict with eternal stakes should not be made, according to most of my parishioners, in a ceremony that involves anything unusual, risky, or uncomfortable.

"Even before I suggested it, the parents requested immersion," I explained to my bishop. "It had been their former denomination's tradition. I wanted to honor that."

He muttered something uncharitable about Baptists. I hastened to explain, "Oh, these folk hadn't been Baptist; they'd been Greek Orthodox."

Orthodox churches, which make up about one third of the world's Christian community, baptize infants by submerging them, their noses held safely shut, in large fonts.

I'd seen it done several times in Greece and thought it was much more appropriate than a few drips for something as awesome as personal incorporation into the life of the Creator of the universe.

So I came down for an interview with a local congregation that immerses. Infant baptism was, of course, a sticking point between the elders and me. They held out for believers baptism; on the other hand I'm used to baptizing infants under six months. There's so much less of them to get under the water than teenagers or adults.

Practical considerations, however, didn't mean much to the elders at that point in the interview; they claimed the important thing was the baptizee's assent to being born again.

I pointed out that the baptizee had given no assent to being born the first time and by analogy needn't give assent to being born again. The parents took responsibility for both birthings.

They explained to me that I had reached the point where the analogy of baptism as a second birth did what even the best analogies eventually do. It broke down.

They proudly showed me their fiberglass baptistery, pastoral wet-suit, and baptismal gowns. Local streams and ponds, they told me, were too messy and at some times of the year too cold. Besides, using the stream was the way the Baptist church a half mile down the road did it. The church interviewing me was more sophisticated. And more practical.

I argued, probably too vehemently, for a setting as natural as the Jordan River instead of a fiberglass tank and for complete nudity instead of wet-suits and gowns. People were born naked, I insisted, they should be born again naked.

My big mistake was to claim that our society has gotten so used to nudity that no one would be shocked. One of the elders considered that thoughtfully, shook his head, and whispered something privately to the others. They agreed to get back to me. They haven't yet.

While I'm waiting to hear from them, if there are any other churches in this paper's range interested in calling an ecumenically minded pastor . . . (Alert R. K. Bohm at: bohmhome@shentel.net)

- - - - -

During a brief interim in Hanover, Penna., I needed to write a spot for the church's April newsletter. After Easter I was planning to do an evening Bible Study series called "What's Next?" and discuss the varied views the Bible has about life after death. So for Easter and as a come-on for the Bible study I wrote a short newsletter piece and then expanded it into the following Easter editorial.

- - - - -

Easter Disappointment
NVD April 15, 2006

Jesus' Easter morning reappearance disappoints me. Not the fact that he came back. I rejoice in that and celebrate it exuberantly.

What disappoints me is Jesus' hardhearted refusal to say anything about the three days between his last breath and his resuscitation. I say it's hardhearted because someday I'll unfortunately breathe my last and I'd really like to know what's in store for me afterwards. But Jesus doesn't tell me.

Tales of after death experiences abounded in Jesus' day. In the Odyssey, the popular Greek epic known by everyone, Ulysses summoned up the spirits of the dead and then had a glimpse into the dark kingdom and observed the punishment of Tantalus and Sisyphus. In Rome's national epic poem Aeneas enters the realm of the dead and describes in detail the River Styx and boatman Charon, the guardian dog Cerberus, the tortures of the wicked, and the Isles of the blessed. Hercules, Orpheus, Theseus, Dionysus, Adonis, all starred in journeys into death replete with details of the geography of the afterlife.

All of them are of course myths. But they are attempts to satisfy the very real curiosity people had and have about what comes next. Jesus had an excellent opportunity to satisfy that curiosity. Alas, either he didn't take advantage of it or the disciples neglected to pass on what he said.

Culminating in Dante's extensive descriptions of the Inferno, Purgatory, and Paradise, medieval Christian literature is also full of stories of what awaits us beyond the grave. They are recaps and adaptations, however, of the old pagan legends and not rooted in anything said by Jesus, or by the rest of the Bible for that matter.

Today too there are ample first-hand descriptions of near-death or post-death experiences. Everyone is familiar with them: the awareness of coming out of the body, the bright light, the gathering of former family members and friends, the sense of deep peace and contentment. If that's actually what it's like I wish Jesus had said so. If the record reported Jesus giving that kind of description I'd be more likely to believe it. As it is I have to pit those modern, Johnny-and-Jill-come-lately accounts against Jesus' own silence. If that's really what it's like, why didn't Jesus say so? I'd trust his report.

Instead of describing his experience after dying, the resurrected Jesus is reported only to have talked about remobilizing his understandably disheartened followers. None of them seems to have asked "What was death like?" If someone did and he answered, the answer wasn't recorded. My suspicion is that in all the whirlwind of excitement and renewed motivation either the disciples didn't have a chance to ask or, if they did, Jesus never bothered to answer.

What did the resurrected Jesus say to his disciples instead of describing the hours after his death?

Mark's oldest manuscripts leave off abruptly with the women leaving the empty tomb and saying nothing to anyone because they were frightened. Later manuscripts of Mark add differing conclusions not in Mark's style and apparently summaries of the conclusions in the other gospels.

Matthew reports the risen Jesus commissioning his followers to go and make disciples, teaching them to observe Jesus' commandments: caring for the poor and needy, working for justice and peace.

In Luke Jesus sends his followers to call all people to repentance and forgiveness: sorrow for their past misdeeds and a new start with a better lifestyle.

John's gospel has the resurrected Jesus in Jerusalem commissioning his followers to do what he had been doing: "As the father sent me, even so I send you,' with special emphasis on being agents of forgiveness. In an appearance in Galilee Jesus three times commands Peter, as the leader of the disciples, to feed the sheep and lambs, that is, to provide for those in any need.

All four accounts, even Mark, are full of the reassurance, "Don't be afraid!", the repeated verb "Go! Go! Go!", and the assurance that Jesus' followers will be empowered to carry out their task.

"Live, and carry on my mission" is the consistent message from the one who burst out of the tomb. And, by implication from his silence about it: "Don't worry about death."

Maybe in fact it's for the best that the resurrected Jesus didn't bother talking about what death is like. How much more important than knowing what's in store for me afterwards to know how my life can be lived most divinely here and now.

- - - - -

The next two editorials began as one, combining a review of how the Bible was transmitted by copying through the centuries with an account of how the separate books of the Christian section came together. Too much material for one essay, it needed to be divided into two. In some ways both articles are very academic and might consequently prompt the question "Who cares?" My experience with many different Bible study groups from Catasauqua, Pennsylvania, to Strasburg, Virginia, indicates, however, a real hunger for this kind of background information. After I've presented it to the satisfaction of these groups I've always had to field the angry question, "Why didn't somebody tell us this before?" So here it is in another form.

- - - - -

Believe Which Bible?
NVD May 13, 2006

"Believe the Bible, Pastor!" some of my more conservative parishioners advise me.

Naturally I do believe the Bible, just as I believe other friends whom I trust. But just as with other friends, I don't believe everything in the Bible unthinkingly and unquestioningly.

(I try to distinguish between what is intended in a literal sense and what might be a metaphor or overstatement. So when Jesus says "I am the vine, you are the branches" I don't look to see where I might be growing leaves or tendrils any more than I look for hardening surfaces if a friend says to me, "You've been a real rock." And when Jesus says "If you're right eye offends you, pluck it out" I don't start looking for something to pry with any more than I look for a shift lever if a friend tells me I'd better get my spindly butt in gear.)

Sometimes when I'm advised "Believe the Bible, Pastor!" I respond, "Which Bible?" "There is only one," they try to reassure me.

But they're wrong, unfortunately misled by Gutenberg's wonderful fifteenth century innovation in the field of publication, moveable type. Although it was a major asset to Bible Study, it also led to a false impression.

As an asset, copies of the Bible mass produced by moveable type became easily available to those families who had neither the time to make their own copies nor the money to pay someone to make a copy for them. Those folks were already familiar with the Bible from hearing the daily or weekly readings in the local churches or cathedrals that were major centers of their social life. They saw Bible stories depicted in stained glass windows and frescos as well as in popular dramas like those of the Corpus Christi processions.

Once people had their own copies they had much more of a sense of ownership. It was now really their book, to review the readings from morning mass, to read on to see what came next, to enjoy discovering passages that weren't included in the church's cycle of public readings.

Mass produced copies of the Good Book, however, also easily gave rise to the popular misunderstanding that there was just one Bible. All printed copies, after all, were exactly alike.

But for fifteen hundred years Bibles had been copied by hand and no two were alike. Even in very careful copying mistakes invariably slipped in, and sometimes when monks were making copies as penance, words, sometimes whole lines, were accidentally skipped or miscopied. Or instead of copying attentively they wrote familiar passages from memory, memories that were sometimes faulty. Sometimes the handwriting being copied was strange or blurred and they copied wrong. Sometimes they thought comments written in the margin belonged in the body of the text and wrote them in. No two handwritten Bibles are therefore alike.

Generally the older the Bible, the less variant readings are in the text. A fifth century manuscript is more trustworthy than a twelfth century manuscript that is the result of a seven hundred year history of copies of copies of copies.

Usually it's easy enough by comparing Bibles to decide which among variant readings was in fact what was written by Mark, John, or Paul three hundred years before our first surviving copies: misspellings, repeated words, dropped words, unusual additions. Sometimes, however, it's difficult. Sometimes it's impossible to decide.

Different Bibles, for example, report the angels' Christmas eve cantata differently. The Bibles authorized by King James in 1611 have "On earth peace, good will toward men." (Luke 2:14) King James' scholars were basing the translation on only a handful of more recent copies of the Greek Bible. The Revised Standard Version was written after the discovery of three important fourth century Biblical manuscripts. Two of the three read "On earth peace toward men of good will." (In the Greek the word order isn't important and the difference is of only one letter.")

On the basis of the Bibles I have no idea which form of the angels' Christmas carol I should believe is the one they sung.

Some of the oldest Bible copies have the story of the woman taken in adultery (John 7:53-8:11), others do not. Was it written by John and accidentally dropped from some later copies? Taken out deliberately as too light on adultery? Added to the text by someone other than John? Which should I believe?

Some of the oldest Bible texts have Jesus at his farewell Passover bless the cup first and then the bread; others have him bless first the cup, then the bread, then a second cup. Which should I believe?

Believe the Bible? Indeed! On the basis of the Bible I continue to believe that a powerful and benevolent Will created everything, has expectations of human beings and holds us accountable, and overcame the strength of evil in all its forms through the death and resurrection of Jesus. But some of the lesser details are blurred. God may be perfect, but the various editions of the Book about God are at points neither flawless nor totally trustworthy.

(bohmhome@shentel.net)

- - - - -

Biblical Technology
NVD June 3, 2006

Technological changes in the fourth century made a very significant impact on the Bible. Before then, in fact, there was no "Bible" as one bound book. The "books" of the Bible were written each on an individual scroll and the scrolls stored in a kind of basket. Jewish synagogues preserve that older tradition and for official worship read from Torah scrolls.

"What'll we read this week?" the leader of an informal, local house fellowship would ask, before church buildings were built.

"We haven't read that passage about love from Paul's letter to Corinth for a while; let's hear that," someone would respond. And out of the basket would be drawn the Corinth scroll.

In the fourth century it was discovered that binding separate pages into book form made the texts much more manageable than scrolls. Instead of unrolling one huge scroll – imagine unrolling from Genesis to Revelation! – all you had to do was flip pages! All the individual scrolls, the five books of Torah, the books of megilloth, the letters of Paul, the other letters, and biographies of Jesus, could be assembled and bound into one volume. What an improvement!

Medieval church art sometimes recalls this tradition. For example, at St. Clement in Rome an apse mosaic shows the Hebrew prophets holding scrolls; opposite them are depicted the evangelists, carrying books, even though they too wrote on scrolls. Their anachronistic bearing of bound books was an artistic device to differentiate them from the prophets.

As often happens, the new technology, while solving one problem, created another. In this case the problem was which of the scrolls from the various baskets of different congregations should be bound together in an Official Book.

Scrolls of books from the Hebrew Bible that counted as divine scripture had already been set by the rabbis. But the Christian congregations had different collections. They had various letters: Paul's, Peter's, Clement's. Most congregational baskets had the traditional four biographies of Jesus, Matthew, Mark, Luke, and John; some added others, such as a Gospel of Peter, or a Gospel of Mary Magdalene, of Thomas or of Philip.

By the fourth century most congregations seemed to have copies of Paul's letters, which of course had originally been written and sent to specific locales: Rome, Corinth, Laodicea. It could have been that congregations exchanged copies of the letters on their own. The Rome congregation, for example, knowing that the Corinth congregation had letters from Paul, wrote or sent messengers to say "We'll show you ours if you show us yours." And thus copies of Paul's letters, each on a separate scroll, found their way around the empire.

Another possibility is that someone intentionally went around collecting, copying, and distributing Paul's letters so that as many congregations as possible would have access to them. Best candidate for having done this was Onesimus.

Whatever the process was, Paul's letter to the Laodiceans, whose circulation to other churches he encourages in Colossians 4:16, never made it into enough baskets to be included in the final, book form edition.

Binding the scrolls by pages into one book raised the question, "Which scrolls should we include? The Gospel of the Egyptians? The Epistle of Barnabas?"

Different congregations, though they had the same basic list, had local variations. As a result some early bound Bibles didn't include all the books of our current Bible; some added books, like the Epistle of Clement which appears in Codex Alexandrinus or the Shepherd of Hermas, in Codex Sinaiticus. And some had the books in a different sequence, like the epistles of Paul after those of James, Peter, and John instead of before.

Collections in the western part of the Roman empire tended to avoid Hebrews, that anti-Jewish book falsely attributed to Paul. Congregations in the eastern part of the Roman empire tended to avoid Revelation, that weird and wonderful surrealistic production that is so often relied upon but misunderstood in some modern church circles.

Eventually there grew up a consensus on which books would be considered "official." No bishop, no council, no theologian made the final decision. It happened by an empire-wide group process among the scattered congregations, one assumes under the guidance of the Holy Spirit.

Of course a few people erroneously believe that the Bible dropped down out of heaven, all sixty-six books pre-assembled into one volume, possibly even in King James English. But if that were in fact the case, how dull in comparison to the real story! (Responses are welcome at bohmhome@shentel.net)

- - - - -

In the sixties there were three very liturgically proper Lutheran congregations in the greater Philadelphia area where members made the sign of the cross. I fell in with them and, because I talk with my hands a lot anyway, picked up the practice. Since then many more Lutheran congregations have begun to make use of the gesture.

My teaching stint at New York Theological Seminary also provided background for this editorial. Almost one half of the students were Baptists, who regularly raised their hands during prayer; another half were Episcopalians, who made the sign of the cross. During worship each group watched the other with a mix of curiosity and suspicion. Little by little some of the Baptists began to make the sign of the cross and some of the Episcopalians began to raise their hands in prayer. It was good to see them learn from one another.

- - - - -

Hand Work in the Church
NVD June 10, 2006

Probably I shouldn't have done it. I knew some people get irritated by it. Beginning a worship service as a supply preacher in a local Lutheran church I made the sign of the cross. Some members responded with the sign of the hostile glare.

Although in some regions Lutheran congregations are used to seeing or using that gesture, in other regions they are not. And a few folk invariably react negatively and complain "I don't like it; it's what Roman Catholics do."

Roman Catholics also stand to hear the Gospel lesson, but I've never heard Lutherans who object to the sign of the cross object to doing that in their services every Sunday. I suspect they don't know it's a Roman Catholic tradition. Don't tell!

I began to muse about gestures: handshakes, head nodding, farewell waves, thumbs up, V for peace, and the one finger gesture of which speeding truckers are often the recipients, deservedly. Humanity talks with its hands regularly and might as well do it as a religious expression too.

Motion forehead to sternum, then shoulder to shoulder can be a reminder of the vertical descent of the Divine to intersect with humanity followed by the horizontal direction of outreach in love or service.

Sketching the cross can be a reminder that as for our sake Jesus took upon himself the cross and its suffering, so we need to be willing for others' sakes to take upon ourselves a cross of suffering and bear patiently and charitably the others' foibles or flaws, shortcomings or sins, whatever irritates or pains us.

Like a plus sign, the imposed cross can be a reminder that God places on each person a positive value, that the divine Gaze sees in each person not something negative or neutral, but something of worth.

Head to chest, arm to arm can be a reminder that God's love shown through the cross needs to touch both our minds and our hearts and then find expression in our actions.

Actually folk who make the sign of the cross probably aren't thinking about what it means. But that's true also of handshakes. Who stops to think "I shall now extend my hand to show that it is empty of a sword and therefore indicates trust and friendship"? Handshakes are just done as the proper gesture associated with greeting someone without thinking about their meaning.

Some Christian worship traditions use the sign of the cross. Other Christians have other gestures. Raising hands in prayer or praise is a common gesture in certain congregations that wouldn't be caught dead making the sign of the cross. It's another meaningful gesture even if its practitioners don't consciously think about its varied meanings as they're doing it: uplift, outreach, openness, vulnerability, even a hint of imitation of Jesus' extending his hands on the cross in love and surrender.

In some Roman Catholic

churches in recent decades it's become not just the priest but some of the members as well who extend and raise their hands during the Lord's Prayer. (Shy ones and beginners tend to keep their extended hands at waist level.) It's good to see the gesture making its appearance there; it should make visiting worshippers from the hand raising tradition feel right at home. Soon maybe those in the hand raising tradition will supplement that gesture with the sign of the cross.

Signing the cross or raising the hands are religious gestures with which I'm comfortable. There is, however, a religious gesture that makes me uncomfortable. It's common, I understand, not just in my own Lutheran circles but across the ecumenical spectrum. Involving the elevation and drop of the shoulders, it's the sign of the shrug.

Ask members if they're willing to serve on council, consistory, vestry, or board of deacons, ask them if they tithe or are moving towards tithing, ask them what they are doing to promote Christian unity or to counter anti-Semitism, and four out of five will respond with the sign of the shrug.

At least they don't respond with the normal gesture of bewilderment and simply scratch their heads.

Making the cross or elevating the hands, kneeling or genuflecting, even hopping or kicking are all gestures that indicate involvement and response of the whole person and have appropriate places in the worship traditions. But the gestures that are probably most important to the divided people who follow Jesus are any gestures of good will that reach across the lines of division. (Responses are welcome at bohmhome@shentel.net.)

- - - - -

Media attention goes so often to what I would consider the more fringe aspects of the Bible or Christianity while the main messages, repeated and emphasized, God's covenant with Abraham and Sarah, the 613 commandments, and Jesus' resurrection, are ignored and overlooked. The "number of the beast" is mentioned only one time, and that in a book that nearly wasn't included as one on the final list of "official" texts. But what a fuss!

Number of Beasts
NVD June 17, 2006

June 6, '06 prompted a large media fuss about "666" as the "number of the beast" from Revelation 13:18. Articles and editorials often identified the "beast" with the "antichrist" in 1 John 2:18-19; 4:3. The identification provides a striking picture: a bestial figure that arises out of the earth, subjugates nations, breathes life into an idol, belches evil spirits like frogs (16:13), and engages in the grand, grandiose, and final battle between good and evil.

Although the beast is obviously opposed to Christ, I have never understood why certain Christian groups have assumed that the "beast" and the "antichrist" mentioned in John's first letter are the same, but they certainly have managed to sell the identification to the media. The reason for that identification is yet another area in which my seminary training seems to have been weak.

My seminaries did review the Book of Revelation, claiming that its prophecies deal not with our day, but, as the author himself says (Rev. 1:-3; 22: 6, 7, 12, 20), with his own era and the overthrow of the totalitarian and oppressive Roman empire, depicted in bizarre but striking symbols like the whore of Babylon (Rev. 17: 3-6) riding on a beast and drunk with the blood of the martyrs, who morphs into the city of Rome, stretched out across seven hills (Rev. 17: 9, 18). They pointed out also that in the thirteenth chapter of Revelation there are actually two beasts, not just one. I often wonder if the first beast, who arises out of the sea (Rev. 13: 1) is disappointed because all the public attention goes to the second beast, whose number is 666, and who arose not out of the sea but out of the earth (Rev. 13: 11).

My seminaries also reviewed the first Letter of John, which has none of the extravagant and shifting imagery that makes Revelation both very colorful and very confusing. John in the first chapter of his Gospel had described Jesus as an incarnation of God's creative power; in the next to last chapter John has Thomas address Jesus flat out as "My Lord and my God," a bold form of address found in no other gospel. Apparently some had taken this to an extreme and were going around denying that there was anything human about Jesus Christ (1 John 2:22; 4:2-3; 2 John 7). Human teachers, not a fantastic beast, who deny "that Jesus Christ has come in the flesh" are following "the spirit of the antichrist, of which you have heard that it is coming; and now it is already in the world" (1 John 4: 2-3). John even remarks that "many antichrists have already come" (1 John 2:18). Not one bestial antichrist at a later time, but many, in John's own day.

Contrasts abound between John's antichristian teachers and Revelation's apocalyptic monster, but in popular thought they are often assimilated nonetheless. This comes as yet another reminder that how the Bible is interpreted is as important as what the Bible says.

Recent hype about 666 joins The DaVinci Code hoopla, documentaries on The Gospel of Judas, the recent creationism debate and hearing in Dover, PA, and discussions of a marriage amendment, raising further questions about how the Bible is properly used and interpreted. Most vocal in all of this seem to be two extremes: those who accept the Bible literally in all aspects as totally without error and those who think the Bible is an antiquated document, perhaps with some interesting features, but certainly not divinely inspired and probably not as worth reading in public schools as Shakespeare is.

Mainline denominations in their public statements and seminary classes do not go to either extreme but take a middle ground, believing the Bible is indeed the inspired Word of God and certainly the divine norm for Christian faith and life, but not considering it literally true in all its statements and totally without error in matters of the churches' proclamation, faith, and life, but not in matters of history, science, and paleontology. Most of them also avoid the conflation of the beast and the antichrist. (Responses are welcome at: bohmhome@shentel.net).

- - - - -

For this one the *Northern Virginia Daily* composed a much better headline that I had, so much better I won't even repeat what mine had been.

- - - - -

The Rights Stuff
NVD June 23, 2006

I mused about all the rights to which folk currently lay claim: animal rights, women's rights, civil rights, gay rights, abortion rights, privacy rights, a right to a speedy trial, a right to be safe from unlawful search or seizure, a right to carry arms, a right to medical assistance, a right to an equal education.

Growing up I heard mentioned among our unalienable rights the right to life, liberty, and the pursuit of happiness. Since that time rights have certainly proliferated. I'm intrigued to imagine what strange new rights will be claimed in the next twenty years. "Plant rights" will probably join "animal rights."

"Rights" are official entitlements or legitimate expectations. Someone may expect to be compensated financially for having returned a lost wallet. "I'm entitled to a reward! I have a right to it!" But it's not a legitimate expectation unless the finder knows the wallet owner has promised a reward.

Someone may claim she is entitled to three weeks vacation – "After all I've done for this firm I have a right to it!" – but it's not official unless the boss acknowledges it.

Any "right" can be granted only by someone who has the official or legitimate authority. I can grant to a neighbor, for example, a "right of way" over land legally mine because I have authority over that land. But I can't grant a right of way over someone else's land. That wouldn't be right.

My other neighbors, working together as a common group called the state, can override my rights to my property and insist that I grant a twenty foot right of way for public use even if I don't want to.

Who has the authority to grant a particular set of rights? In some cases, as with the grant of a right of way, an individual. In many cases the right is or can be granted, implicitly or explicitly, by the government or society:

Altar Ego Musings

women's right to vote, the right to a trial by a jury of peers, the right to equal education. And, as the framers of the Bill of Rights asserted, in some particular cases we may be endowed with certain inalienable rights by our Creator, who has a definite stake in defining rights and wrongs. One problem is we don't all agree on what our Creator expects.

Those terms "endowed" and "inalienable" may have been what muddied the waters and led people to believe that any right they can mention is "built in," part of our natural endowments as our noses or toes, "inalienable," something that cannot be stripped away or lost, and a condition exactly the way the Creator of all things wants it to be. Consider how often all kinds of rights are bolstered with rhetoric that describes them as "God given." For some of those claims I suspect the divine eyebrows might rise in surprise.

Even those rights mentioned in the Bill of Right's preamble as "inalienable" are in fact not inalienable.

That "inalienable" right to life can be lost if society through its governing laws agrees that capital punishment, the death penalty, is appropriate for certain crimes.

That "inalienable" right to liberty is forfeited if imprisonment is the agreed upon punishment for our violation of certain laws.

And we may have the "inalienable" right to pursue happiness all we want to, but only provided the pursuit doesn't involve using substances the majority of our society has agreed shouldn't be used or by thrashing the daylights out of someone we don't like or by propelling our cars at seventy miles an hour in any area where anything above thirty-five is unsafe.

Perhaps better than using the term "right" would be use of the term "permission" or "expectation." The rights to life, liberty, and the pursuit of happiness, the right to bear arms and the right to be free from unwarranted search and seizure are things we can expect, whatever role our Creator may have had in the process, by our mutual agreement as a society to permit or support those things.

"I have a right to . . ." means I have permission or I can legitimately expect certain things to happen or to be prevented. And the question can easily be raised "Who granted that permission?" or "Why do you have that expectation?" in the hopes that the answer won't be a really unanswerable claim: "our Creator." I hope our Creator doesn't subsequently get blamed for too many weird new permissions. (Responses welcome at: bohmhome@shentel.net)

- - - - -

On the one hand church involvement declines nationally; on the other hand there seems to be widespread interest in what can be considered spiritual phenomena: meditation and contemplation, talking to the dead, predicting the future. "Spiritual advisors" was not a category in the Yellow Pages twenty-five years ago; it is now. And for a while in the late nineties when this editorial was written, although not recently, there was a television ad for a psychic advisor hotline. Skeptical, I tried to guess how it might work and my conclusion, presented here, first appeared in my mystery novel, *Testing the Spirits*, in which a Lutheran pastor and a New Age shop owner become allies when their two establishments are both vandalized with graffiti.

- - - - -

On the Psychic Hotline
NVD June 27, 2006

Psychic hotlines rouse my suspicions although I'm a clergyman and presumably should be very open – some folks would say very gullible – when it comes to supernatural or spiritual matters. I'm especially skeptical when the Tarot card reader in the TV ad has an accent that flits confusingly back and forth between Jamaican and Irish.

Skepticism, after all, is part of my religious tradition, in which a skeptical apostle who challenged the claim that Jesus had risen could also be a saint: doubting Thomas.

As a clergyman I'm often like Thomas, challenging claims and questioning beliefs, both my own and others: Could it be true? What other explanations are possible? Does this contradict other things I know about the world or myself? Can those contradictions be resolved?

How?

Naturally I question the psychic hotline phenomenon too. I am automatically suspicious of anything that makes life easier to cope with or simpler to understand. Like fundamentalism for example.

Recently while I was questioning the possibility of psychic hotlines I had a revelation that nearly made me a true believer. My son in Washington, D.C., briefly showed psychic powers himself.

I had telephoned him to share some important news at a time of day I would never normally call. He picked up the phone and immediately said, "Hi, Dad!"

He knew it was I even before he answered. I congratulated him on his psychic powers and bubbled over with plans for going into business together: I'd be his manager and promoter and arrange for him to receive phone calls from movie stars and sports figures, all ready to pay enormous sums of money for him to tell them what's wrong with their love lives.

"Dad," he interrupted my bubbling over. "I don't have psychic powers. I have caller ID on the telephone."

Bubbles burst. My temporary willingness to believe yielded to skepticism once again, and I resigned myself to being a poor parish pastor for a few more decades. Unless . . .

I could set myself up as a psychic. I'm even ordained and can thus officially use the title "Reverend." When someone calls me, even before I answer the phone I use caller ID to find out who it is and where the call is coming from. I hop on my computer's information superhighway while doing initial chit-chat with the caller: "I'm arranging the Tarot cards now . . ." Meanwhile my internet connection provides me a wealth of information: Where the person is calling from (cross check local news from that area) and what his financial history has been. Legal records, school records, business records. I wonder how much I could learn in how short a time? Probably enough to amaze the person with my knowledge.

I may not actually have psychic powers, but if I ever want an alternate to being a poor parish pastor, I know how to make it seem as if I do.

Of course I'm not saying that's how psychic hotlines really work.

Probably, or at least possibly – well, maybe – the popular Hollywood stars, big name athletes, or former presidents' wives who swear by psychic advisors are far too smart to be duped into endorsing anything so obvious.

But as a clergyman I'm able to bring myself to believe all kinds of things: creation from nothing, deliverance of Sarah and Abraham's offspring from Egypt, return of Jesus from three days in death, the eventual victory of a kingdom of righteousness and justice. And I could probably bring myself to believe even that psychic hotlines are nothing more than a manifestation of the miracle of computer technology. (For a personal reading, consult: bohmhome@shentel.net)

I'm in a bind. I agree with much of what is labeled "politically correct." And on the other hand I think much of what is labeled "politically correct" is foolishness. I wish the term had never been coined. But since it has been I thought I should deal with it.

Politically Correct
NVD July 1, 2006

"Politics" and its variant forms seem to have become bad words, especially the phrase "politically correct." I don't need to muse very much to decide why that is. Recent politicians have given politics a very disreputable reputation.

Consequently, accusations that a legislator has said or done something "for political reasons" has come to sound as if it had been said or done for underhanded reasons, for nefarious reasons, for mean spirited reasons.

Of course a person in politics will do something for political reasons! What's unusual or wrong about that? A person in academics does things for academic reasons. A person in commerce does things for commercial reasons. A person in medicine does things for medical reasons. What is wrong if someone in politics does things for political reasons?

What's wrong is the way politics is too often done nowadays: underhandedly, nefariously, and mean spiritedly.

"Politics" is a word that goes back to a Greek term for the business of managing a "polis," a city. Farmers and country folk had the room to do pretty much as they chose. But cram a large number of people into a polis, whether it's a real metropolis or just a cosmopolitan locale, and a large amount of people management will need to be done; laws established and enforced, public buildings erected and maintained, commerce and industry both encouraged and regulated, and all things supervised in such a way that they work together for the common good.

"Politics" was not a dirty word and "for political reasons" did not mean deviously, deceptively or unscrupulously. Fair and noble was politics, the task of managing the polis, in its origin and early stages. Upright and respected were those elected or appointed to do the managing, the politicians. At one time parents would actually be proud – believe it or not – to announce that one of their children was going into politics.

How times change, and terminological associations with them!

One of my parishioners two decades ago, a gruff old curmudgeon who hated to let anyone know he was really a kind, helpful, and caring person underneath it all, once took me thoroughly aback at a Bible study by prefacing his remark with "Now I don't want to seem like a do-gooder." So taken aback was I that I don't remember the actual point he went on to make, though twenty years later I still recall the astounding preface.

"Why wouldn't a Christian want to seem like a do-gooder?" I mused. "We're supposed to be do-gooders. What is the problem with letting it show?"

Eventually I realized that he wasn't expressing disapproval of doing good. He was trying to distance himself from the crowd of namby-pamby, showy, self righteous do gooders who always sound trumpets when they give alms or say prayers.

I suspect it works the same way with the term "political." Because so many political figures have given the political process a bad name people want to distance themselves as far as possible from anything involving the term "politics." Of all things, they don't even want to admit to being "politically correct" any more than my parishioner wanted to admit to being a "do gooder"

Muse with me about it. Have you ever heard the phrase "politically correct" used in a positive sense? Isn't "politically correct" always used disparagingly?

Muse about it some more. By wholesale denigration of "political correctness" people are tacitly approving being politically incorrect! They're making it sound as if the correct thing to do is not to work for what is supposed to be good for the polis but to work against it.

I'm well aware that much of what is intended to come under the umbrella of "politically correct" is in fact blatant blither or nattering nonsense, social fads rather than serious laws, trendy tendencies rather than judicial adjudications. Even so, what intrigues me is the negative connotation in the use of the term "politically correct."

To be "politically correct" should mean to be well informed about political candidates, political discourse, and the political process as well as to be well involved with voicing an opinion, voting, and volunteering.

Alas, being "politically correct" has come to mean to do something everyone seems interested in resisting. Being "politically incorrect" has become the ideal! Many (most?) of our politicians must be happy with that situation. They can feel right at home. (Cast your vote at bohmhome@shentel.net)

- - - - -

A summer heat wave reminded me of my winter editorial about snow and I did the following for the hell of it. It was the swiftest publication I have had. Submitted by e-mail shortly after noon on Tuesday, it was in the Northern Virginia Daily in my delivery box before dawn the next day.

- - - - -

Hot as Hell? Maybe Even Hotter
NVD August 2, 2006

"Hot as hell, isn't it, Pastor?" parishioners asked me during the current heat wave.

Actually I'm no expert on the nether regions and their climatology, and I hope I never become one by first-hand experience. Nor, coming out of a Lutheran tradition, do I normally preach hell-fire and brimstone (KJV) or sulfur (RSV) sermons, although given the condition of contemporary society, maybe I should start.

"How hot is hell?" I mused in response to the question.

Not very, according to Dante's classic description in the *Inferno*, the first section of his Italian epic from 1300, followed by *Purgatorio* and *Paradiso*. There Dante follows the pagan Latin poet, Vergil, deep down into the earth through ten circles of hell, most of whose features are borrowed not from the Bible, but from the underworld descent in the sixth book of Vergil's *Aeneid*. At the lowest circle Dante discovers not fire and flame, but ice. Satan, at the heart of hell, is in fact embedded to his chest in ice.

Dante's title, "*Inferno*," has an interesting history. From the Latin, it means "down under" – *pace* Australians – is related to "infra" and "inferior," and has nothing to do with fire or flames. It has acquired the secondary meaning of a raging conflagration because "down under" was popularly thought to be the everlasting fires, no matter how much ice Dante envisioned there.

Of course, it could be that medieval Italian poets are simply not to be trusted, especially when they're guided and influenced by pagan Latin writers.

And of course it could be that descriptions of hell and heaven, non-physical, spiritual realms, must employ physical terms with a poetic, non-literal sense and therefore may vary from writer to writer. Whether hell is described physically as too hot or too cold, the point is that it isn't a comfortable abode but will be an eternal pain in whatever passes for parts of our anatomy once we are beyond our bodies.

Scripture doesn't have nearly as detailed a geography (hadesology?) as Dante. The lake of fire and sulfur into which are thrown Satan and the wicked to be tormented forever and ever is always popular with some Christian groups, although the book of Revelation in which it appears, chapter twenty, nearly wasn't accepted into the New Testament book.

Fire for burning weeds or raining down on Sodom and Gomorrah were popular images in Jesus' day used not for what happens after the end of the world but for what will happen at the end of the world (Matt. 13: 40-42, Luke 17:29, 2 Peter 3: 7-13, and Jude 7). Maybe it's assumed the fire burns on below after the "new heaven and new earth" are revealed.

Jesus himself says nothing about fire in lake form, but does mention "the fire prepared for the devil and his angels "(Matt. 25:41) and Lazarus being "in an agony in this flame." He also refers to "Gehenna, where the worm never dies and the fire is never quenched" (Mark 9:44). "Gehenna," Jerusalem's garbage dump, was a popular metaphor for unpleasant places. How far should its literal meaning of worms and fire be pushed?

Jesus seems to prefer threats of being thrown "into outer darkness, where there will be weeping and gnashing of teeth" (Matt. 8:12, 22:13, etc.). "Outer" and "darkness" and pain references can be more frightening than the fire image, especially in winter.

Normally I don't preach that disasters, natural or human, are sent by God as signs or punishment. I would not preach, for example, that 9/11 was God's reaction to America's increasing openness to same-sex couples; I would not preach that Katrina's destruction of New Orleans was a divine housecleaning event similar to Sodom and Gomorrah.

If, however, recent reports in the newspapers and on television are right that the heat wave was an aspect of global warming, then I indeed can see it as a sign and punishment of human greed and gluttony and insistence on comfort at all costs. Gas guzzling vehicles and industrial plants and electric companies spewing excess carbon dioxide into the air to keep up with, among other things, air conditioners cranked to the maximum are only some of the factors that are turning up the heat on humanity, with or without divine intervention.

"Hot as hell, isn't it, Pastor?" Indeed! Maybe because we've been misbehaving. (Responses welcome: bohmhome@shentel.net)

A member from St. Mark, Hanover, asked me on a home visit how I felt about "other gods." Weren't they all the same? He had worked closely with a Muslim man, seen him praying fervently and heard him talk ardently about his faith in Allah. It wasn't an abstract theological question; it was very personal, arising out of love and concern for his friend. I told him I had an editorial for him, but then discovered that it hadn't yet been published although it had been written and submitted much earlier. I printed off an advance copy for him. I think his concern is shared by many and I was glad when it appeared in the *Daily* a month later.

- - - - -

Differing Views of God
NVD August 12, 2006

"It's all the same God," people often tell me. And I can say a heartfelt "Yes" or "Amen" when they mean the god worshipped by my Lutheran congregation and their own Presbyterian or Methodist or Roman Catholic or Seventh Day Adventist congregation. Each of us does have different views of the Supreme Power: the god of Roman Catholics insists on celibate clergy; the god of Lutherans does not; the god of Disciples of Christ restricts baptism to those who consent; the god of Episcopalians welcomes infants into the waters. But within the Christian family of faith, we're pretty much agreed that we worship the same God, though we admit some branches of the family have weird ideas about her, or him.

"There's just one God," sometimes, however, also means, for those who make the claim, that the god worshipped by Muslims is the same as the one worshipped by the Hindus, and that Sheva and Mahadeva, Apollo and Dionysus, are all the same.

"Could that be?" I mused.

Not according to Christian theologians. (I wonder if there's a group term for Christian theologians, as there is "gaggle of geese", "pod of whales," "glory of nightingales." I'd suggest "a plague of theologians." Don't tell my bishop!)

I suspect that on this matter the people are right and the plague of theologians is wrong, innocently and subconsciously motivated by their desire to keep their domain exclusive.

How could strikingly different deities actually be the same?

Imagine a woman who is a wife, a mother, a lawyer, and a beekeeper hobbyist being described by those who know her only in those different contexts. Her legal clients would, we would hope, know and consequently say nothing about her remarkable sexual prowess, one of the first things her husband would think of about her, though he might not talk about it. His children and he would be able to say she regularly changed the oil in the family cars; her legal clients, used to seeing her in a business suit, prim, proper and professional, might find the picture of her feet sticking out from under a car and grease smears on her forehead impossible to accept. Her friends from beekeeper society meetings have no clue that she's a mother and an excellent lawyer, though from her wedding band they've deduced that she's married. They'd describe her as rather easy going; her children, in contrast, would argue "Too strict!" None of them would know about the unusual incident in eleventh grade that she kept completely secret. Except, of course, for the other two girls involved. And all of the others would be shocked if they heard about it and would respond, "That doesn't sound like her!"

Different contexts, different relationships, and very different perspectives or images of the same person.

Of course with the woman in our analogy there is the common denominator of physical appearance among all the people who know her. All of them, however different their descriptions of her might be, would agree "That's her!" if they actually saw her. With an unseen Power we don't have that opportunity; our descriptions have to be based on non-physical characteristics and in different circumstances, like the lady in our analogy, the Creator will relate very differently and perhaps even seem to behave contradictorily.

The more the beekeepers get to know the woman who is

also a lawyer, the more her clients talk with her, the fuller and more accurate a picture they'll all have. And if they talk with one another – children with clients, husband with beekeepers, and all of them with her eleventh grade friends – she'll be revealed even more fully.

Rather than a theological approach of "my deity is real and yours isn't" or "my deity is better than yours," the best approach to a multiplicity of divinities is to ask, in terms of the analogy, "How does my knowledge of God as beekeeper fit in with your knowledge of God as mother? How is my picture of God as lawyer supplemented by your picture of God as lover?"

Enough conversation and listening might even help the Disciples of Christ and Episcopalians come to a mutually agreeable conclusion about the baptism question. Eventually. (Report your perspective on the deity to: bohmhome@shentel.net.)

- - - - -

I often have ambivalent feelings, which means I can see both sides of an issue. My ambivalent feeling about ethnic jokes, avoiding them because they can be hurtful, enjoying them because they can be funny, works its way towards a resolution here.

- - - - -

Sensitive to Ethnic Jokes
NVD August 19, 2006

"Pastor, did you hear the one about the priest, the rabbi, and the minister?" parishioners often ask me.

"Which one?" I used to be tempted to ask. I'd heard so many clergy jokes, almost as regularly as I hear the one about pastors having it so easy, working only one morning a week. The one that's not very funny.

I also used to say, "No, tell me," in the hope that it would indeed be one I hadn't heard before. Lately, however, I've had serious reservations about encouraging jokes about religions or ethnic groups. I've become sensitive.

It started fifteen years ago. Teaching at New York Theological Seminary, I digressed during a lecture into a black joke. One of my young teaching assistants, a white lad, later took me aside privately and took me to task seriously. He had found my joke in very poor taste and offensive.

"But almost half the class is black and they all laughed," I defended myself.

"They had to," I was solemnly reminded. "You're the teacher."

From then on I've been increasingly reluctant and apprehensive about ethnic jokes.

Being "politically correct?" For all that "political correctness" is disparaged, as I discussed in an earlier column, sometimes the advocates of political correctness do indeed make sense. It is true that jokes at the expense of another person or group can be mocking, demeaning, belittling, rude, and hurtful.

So I have begun to try to be sensitive. When a religious joke is about to be told, for example, I'm cautious out of concern about how my parishioners and I relate with, or to, people different from us. I certainly don't want my parishioners to mock priests and rabbis. Or pastors, for that matter! After all, that would include me.

I remember happier days when jokes about Pennsylvania Germans and Italians, Polish and blonds, Afro-Americans and cripples, were not likely to raise red flags and incur accusations of insensitivity and prejudice.

But on the other hand I'm well aware how hurt and upset people can get when their group is the intended object of derision. Consider the recent reaction to the political cartoon showing a nun and Mel Gibson. Actually I had chuckled at it myself, but only because it's premise verged on the absurd. Some took it seriously and were offended.

On yet another hand, which makes three hands and thoroughly confuses the situation, I remember that some of the fiercest jokes about Roman Catholics were told to me by Roman Catholics. Priests even! And blonds were the ones most often to tell me blond jokes. And the week after the seminary incident three of my black students told me jokes about blacks. (When I reported that to my teaching assistant, he suggested they were gunning for good grades.)

Finally, I muse about the winners of this year's Last Comic Standing on television. In the final round an Afro-American and a man with cerebral palsy told jokes about blacks and cripples with impunity! If I were to crack funny in public the way they did I'd surely be subject to reprimand by more than a mere teaching assistant.

I concluded that jokes about oneself or one's own group, or jokes told in an environment and atmosphere of mutual trust and caring are acceptable. And I suspect that people have become more sensitive today about ethnic jokes because society has become much less mutually trusting and caring than it had once been. We're swifter now to take offense because more people now are prone to be offensive.

When the Kingdom comes, I'm sure it will ring with the boisterous laughter of people enjoying an environment of love and caring in which we'll laugh resoundingly both at our own and also at others' foibles and foolishness. Even before the Kingdom comes, being able to laugh that way with one another without offense can be an advance sign of the Kingdom. But alas, in our fallen condition it isn't always easy or possible to distinguish between laughing with one another supportively and forgivingly and laughing at others derisively and hurtfully. Caution and prudence may be best.

That reminds me! Did you hear the one about the teaching assistant at New York Theological Seminary? (Your clergy jokes are welcome at: bohmhome@shentel.net)

- - - - -

Hastily written to respond to the news that the planet Pluto had been demoted, the following article was an embarrassment. As the former president of both the Lehigh Valley Amateur Astronomical Society and the Shenandoah Astronomical Society I should never have attributed the discovery of the four minor planets in orbit between Mars and Jupiter to Galileo. Galileo discovered the four moons of Jupiter. One of my readers politely called to my attention this oversight, which is a euphemism for "glaring error."

- - - - -

Planetary Changes
NVD August 28, 2006

Degraded! Pluto is no longer one of our traditional nine planets. The International Astronomical Union on August 24 reduced the official number to eight and placed Pluto in a new category: "dwarf planet," which includes Ceres, formerly known as an asteroid or minor planet, and a body recently discovered beyond Pluto and temporarily and unofficially named "Xena," Greek for "Stranger" or "Foreigner."

Changes in tradition always arouse opposition. School text manufacturers are already lamenting their need to redo. And some folk are likely to complain "If nine planets were good enough for Moses and Peter, they're good enough for me!"

Although surely observed by Moses, Peter, and their contemporaries, planets are not referred to in the Bible and no names are given. We use names not from Judeo-Christian revelation but from ancient pagan deities: for the five naked eye planets: Mercury, Venus, Mars, Jupiter, and Saturn, for those discovered later: Uranus, Neptune, and Pluto.

Actually Biblical astronomy was quite different from ours. Earth was pictured stationary at the center of all things with the Sun, Moon, and stars circling around it. In their dark, unpolluted night skies Moses and Peter could indeed watch the planets, bright points of light like stars, drifting back and forth across the fixed, unchanging pattern of the constellations. The word "planet" itself is from a Greek word meaning "wanderer."

See for yourself! Right now (late August, 2006) Jupiter is the bright object moving in front of Scorpius in the southwestern sky in early evening; Mercury, Saturn and Venus are shifting their positions in the northeastern dawn sky.

I've often mused that updating our planetary system would be a good idea for two reasons.

First, it would avoid the obvious religious problem which sooner or later will wind up in the courts. After all, if religion is to be kept out of the public schools we can't have our students looking up to Jupiter or keeping track of Uranus and Neptune or doing reports on the activities of Mars and Venus. As a Lutheran clergyperson I resent that Roman gods and one goddess can get free school publicity, but mine cannot.

Second, renaming could avoid the current, overwhelmingly masculine bias which the traditional planetary names blaze across the skies. Of the traditional nine planets, only one is named for a goddess. Of course, that goddess is Venus herself, who certainly carries more clout than Mercury, Mars, and Saturn put together. And now that there are only eight planets, there s a higher percentage of feminine representation. But even so, feminism is poorly represented.

At least a goddess made it into the new list of "dwarf planets." Ceres, the goddess of cereal, grain, and crops, is the largest of the thousands of asteroids circling the Sun between the orbits of Mars and Jupiter. With her are three other asteroids large enough to have been seen and named by Galileo four centuries ago: Vesta, Juno, and Ganymede. None of them, however, was large enough to be classified with Ceres as "dwarf planet." In some ways that's a shame; they would have added two more female names to the planetary list. Perhaps in another way, however, it's just as well. Ganymede's sexual orientation would certainly give some people pause on its inclusion as planet, regular or dwarf.

Asked "Who was Ganymede?" a teacher would have to tell the story of Jupiter's "involvement" and perhaps even add the etymological note that "catamite" is a variation of "Ganymede." As it is, Ganymede can more easily hide in the closet among the other thousands of asteroids.

By what right, some might ask indignantly, are the heavenly bodies being shuffled around in this way under new designations?

Lurking in the Biblical mandate that humanity should give names to the animals (Genesis 2:19-20) lies not only our task of developing a system of genera and species for use in biology but also the duty of determining the definition of "planet" and their names. The purpose of the Bible is not to teach us science.

In the absence of clear and concrete Biblical guidelines, humanity calls the shots so that when congregations sing a hymn such as "Earth and all stars, loud-rushing planets," the Maker of all must keep in mind, "Oh, they've decided that no longer includes Pluto." (Responses welcome: bohmhome@shentel.net)

- - - - -

I sometimes worry that religious people are not sufficiently critical about religious matters, as I observed in "Tabloid Theology." They so often resist encouragement to be "critical" because they think of it in the negative sense of fault-finding or nit-picking, not in the positive sense of evaluating, doing a critique. Thus, when many religious people see something religious like a billboard signed "God" they accept it as a good thing and don't stop to ask the critical question, "Is this really a good thing?" Consequently in the following editorial I ask the question for them. And answer it too!

- - - - -

God's Billboards
NVD September 2, 2006

"God is writing billboards, Pastor; open the attachment for some examples," happily announced an e-mail from one of my parishioners.

At first I was delighted that the Maker of all things was finally speaking out first-hand and not relying on divine messages being relayed second-hand. God has left, of course, messages in the Bible, but translations are not always completely accurate and sometimes the messages are contradictory: Is it faith alone (Romans 3:28) or are good deeds necessary (James 2:17)?

Preachers, theologians, and laity disagree among themselves about the meaning of God's messages. Even solemn church councils split down the middle on what God says about blessing or ordaining people in certain relationships. Amid the confusion I was eager to learn what was the very word of God that had been written on billboards.

I opened the attachment and began reading.

First was "That 'love thy neighbor' thing – I meant that. – God."

I was pleased. It was a positive message, not like some recent parade posters announcing, erroneously I trust, whom God hates. And its presentation on a billboard meant it was more likely to be seen by people who may not read the original source of the quote in the Bible.

Second was "Come to my House before the game. – God." I was glad about that one too. It showed God as reaching out, establishing contact, longing for fellowship with humanity. I sometimes worry that God doesn't try to do that as much as possible and may even be losing interest in our quarrelsome, cantankerous human race. But I was a little concerned that the message might be misunderstood by those not completely familiar with religious terminology. What if they thought "my House" meant heaven rather than a local synagogue or church? Might it seem to some that God was encouraging committing suicide rather than watching the game?

Religious communications to non-religious folk can be tricky.

Third was "What part of 'thou shalt not' don't you understand? – God." I began to be puzzled. Its belittling tone, definitely not appropriate for one who promoted the theme "love thy neighbor," made it more of a haughty reprimand than a caring encouragement.

Two more signs added to my uncertainty: "You think it's hot now? – God," and "Keep using my name in vain and I'll make gridlock worse. – God."

Alas, those two were likely to reinforce the unfortunate views of some of my atheist friends that the God depicted in Scripture is exceedingly judgmental and vindictive. At least the billboard threat was simply to make rush hour worse and not to wreak some really terrible vengeance on our rebellious race. Then too, threats of gridlock seemed both ineffective and petty.

I was becoming more and more confused. And next I read this message: "Don't make me come down there. – God." What now thoroughly confused me was that it sounded not like an offer to help but like a threat.

I knew that wasn't the kind of thing the God of the Bible would say, as if reluctant and unwilling to come down here and preferring to stay aloof and uninvolved. The God of the Bible manifestly preferred to come down and get involved.

"I have come down to deliver," God said, not on a billboard but in Exodus 3:8. In the face of Egyptian oppression of Israel, God does not look down indifferently but comes down willingly in mercy and compassion to straighten out one of the messes humanity had gotten itself involved in.

Similarly the Christian message is that God didn't stay far above looking down and clucking over human sinfulness and letting gridlock occur in future years, God came down in the person of Jesus, not to punish but to share in experiencing all the suffering, pain, alienation, injustice, and hostility of which humanity can be guilty.

Musing on the billboard messages I came to a startling conclusion! They were not actually written by God's own Self!

How disappointed I was. I realized they were written by some person or group merely claiming to be speaking, or writing, on God's behalf. So naturally the question arose in my mind: Were they presenting God's messages accurately or inaccurately?

I wished again that God would speak out first-hand and not rely on messages being delivered second-hand by Moses or Matthew or Paul or local preachers or popular theologians or billboard writers. Or even editorial authors. (Your message is welcome at: bohmhome@shentel.net)

- - - - -

On September 8 the Northern Virginia daily published the third of the five in my Noah ark series, which I included above rather than here. The next day, September 9, they published my editorial about four letter words. That was the only time I've had editorials appear two days in a row. To anticipate my next article: Hot damn!

- - - - -

Parsing Bad Words
NVD September 9, 2006

Four letter words abound today. I don't mean good ones like love and hope. I mean bad ones, like the 's' word heard from the president's already full mouth at an official and formal dinner party.

Parishioners often lament: "Pastor, our daughter's language

is dreadful; will you talk to her?" or "Pastor, aren't you upset by all the swearing on TV?" or "Pastor, we've stopped going to the movies because of all the cursing."

Taking my pastoral duties seriously, I did indeed encourage the young girl not to use dreadful language. I advised her not to use "like" every four or five words and I reviewed with her the distinctions between "like" and "as," between "who" and "whom," the importance of heeding Kilpatrick's column on English usage and of not emulating the style of many Associated Press writers.

Her puzzled response was, "Pastor, what the hell are you talking about?"

More important to me, however, than trying to improve the dreadful language of our teens, and too many AP writers, is enlightening people over forty, so many of whom just do not understand the distinction between swearing, cursing, blasphemy, profanity, and obscenity. As a result when a younger person utters an obscenity, an older person is likely to say "Stop cursing." Or the response to an instance of blatant blasphemy is "Please don't swear."

With such linguistic confusion it's no wonder our society is in a mess. And indeed I consider the churches and synagogues to blame for not having taught the proper distinctions back in the days when nearly everyone went to church or synagogue. Clergy were probably reluctant for fear they may have to use a four letter word in the pulpit as an example.

Let me set the record straight.

To curse is to imprecate, to invoke the deity to hurt or harm someone, to call down God's ill will or wrath. "God blast you" or its stronger variations is a curse.

I've heard parents respond to their offspring's use of a participle built on a four letter word for intercourse – I don't mean "talk" – with "I wish you wouldn't use so many curse words." I try to explain to the parents the real meaning of "curse."

Their puzzled reply is usually, "Pastor, what the hell are you talking about?"

To swear is to invoke the deity's name in support of the truth of a statement: "So help me God I'm telling the truth" or "As God is my judge" or just "By God." The Nazareth rabbi forbade swearing altogether (Matthew 5:34), which certainly poses a challenge to our normal court procedures.

Blasphemy is saying something untrue or injurious about God. In *Blues Brothers* Aretha Franklin uses it accurately when she yells at Elwood "Don't you blaspheme!" He's just announced that the brothers are on a mission from God and she obviously considers that claim demeaning or disrespectful of God's dignity. (She forgets what a grand variety of other ne'er-do-wells or unlikely candidates God has chosen for divine missions.)

Some might well consider blasphemy those posters that read "God hates certain kinds of people," but that claim seems not to upset as many of my parishioners as do terms for body parts or body functions.

Words for body parts or functions are neither swearing, nor cursing, nor blaspheming. Their category is "obscenity" or "profanity," both of which mean not of acceptable social usage.

One generation's accepted usage is another's obscenity. The original King James Bible had at 1 Kings 16:11 the four letter "p" word for "urinate:" "Everyone who p...eth against a wall." (Actually, with "-eth" it's a seven letter word.) Many modern KJV editions retain the "p" phrase; some, sensitive to modern usage, substitute "Every male." Check your own KJV. Don't be scandalized if it's there; it was a perfectly acceptable term back then. Beware if it is not there: if you can't trust the accuracy of the KJV, which version can you trust?

Words, four letters or otherwise, are neither good nor bad in themselves; they become good or bad by our use of them. The "p" word was not offensive in King James' day; today it offends some folks, others not. Following Paul's advice, we should avoid offending neighbors, or parents, or strangers by using words we know will upset them.

Be sensitive to the impact your choice of words might have on others, lest all hell break loose. (Responses welcome: bohmhome@shentel.net)

God's Will – Or Not?
NVD September 28, 2006

"God wants it that way" is certainly a difficult claim to refute. How can one argue with the Creator of all things? Of course the Creator of all things rarely speaks directly but apparently entrusts the divine messages to underlings to deliver. That's a good way to stay out of heated debate but it certainly complicates things for humanity since it's often difficult to decide which of opposing claims really represents God's will.

It happens on a congregational level when there's a debate about such theologically heated and socially significant topics as changing the time of the worship service or introducing a new hymnal. Or deciding on a building program!

Caught in a bind between antiquated and inadequate facilities and dwindling finances, the congregation debates whether or not to take on an expensive building program.

"God wants us to build so that we can accommodate more people more easily," one person asserts.

"God wants us to invest in others: in community ministry programs and foreign missions, not in bricks and mortar," another insists.

"God wants us to have faith that the money will be there when we need it for whatever purpose."

"God wants us to be sensible, realize our limitations, and not undertake something beyond our capabilities."

How helpful it would be if God did the speaking and didn't leave it up to intermediaries. During those congregational debates I raise my eyes heavenward in frustration and appeal, offering the silent prayer "Intervene! Settle this mess!"

And in the distant corners of my mind at the edge of my consciousness I sometimes seem to hear a very faint voice saying, "You're their pastor! Either help them come to an agreement or decide for them!"

I always assume it's just my imagination so I don't have to tell them "It's God's will either that you come to an agreement or that you do it my way."

It's not just in congregations, however, that we have to rely on secondary spokespersons to hear what God's will is. It happens in the debates in the political arena as well.

God wants us to help the poor and needy by providing them with welfare. God wants us to help the poor and needy by forcing and enabling them to find employment. God wanted us to intervene in Iraq. God never wanted us in Iraq. God wants us to stay the course. God wants us out as soon as possible. God wants to send gays to hell; God wants gays to be accepted. God wants a constitutional amendment defining marriage.

Complicating the situation is the possibility of those claiming to know "God's Will" making an appeal to "God's word," the Bible. But there too we bump into different approaches. Some say, "God's will is for us in all circumstances to believe everything in the Bible;" others say, "God's will is for in some circumstances to use our God-given intelligence to interpret the Bible."

How helpful it would be in such circumstances if God did the speaking and didn't leave it up to intermediaries. During those debates on how to use the Bible I raise my eyes heavenward in frustration and appeal, offering the silent prayer "Intervene! Settle this mess!"

And in the distant corners of my mind at the edge of my consciousness I sometimes seem to hear a very faint voice saying, "Don't put Me in the middle of it!" I always assume it's just my imagination so I don't have to tell them "God doesn't want to take sides."

Maybe it is in fact a good thing that God leaves it to humanity to work together for amicable solutions, like a loving parent who abandons an autocratic and dictatorial role in order to let the siblings settle things amicably on their own.

However the marriage amendment goes in the future, I'm hoping someone proposes an amendment to the constitution that "In my opinion" must always preface any claim to be expressing God's will in order to underline the fact that different people see God's will differently and no one individual or group has a monopoly on understanding the divine Mind. (Responses are welcome: bohmhome@shentel.net)

- - - - -

Having admitted in the previous article to hearing voices "in the distant corners of my mind at the edge of my consciousness," I decided to admit the whole truth in the following editorial, very loosely based on part of a sermon I preached at St. Mark, Mechanicsburg, when the text for the day was the story of Jesus' temptation. I began the sermon by asking "Do any of you hear voices in your heads?" and only a high school junior raised his hand. Members stared at him and whispered to one another. At the end of the sermon I repeated the question and everyone joined the high school junior by raising hands.

- - - - -

Voices in My Head
NYD September 30, 2006

I hear voices in my head! Please don't tell my bishop. My closer friends have, I'm sure, suspected it. Some readers of these columns have hinted that I should be classified with those people who hear voices and need to be put in safe places.

Voices I hear in my head are not always very clear and articulate; often they are muffled and garbled. For example, when another pastor won a local preaching award, the voice was not very distinct but seemed vaguely to be saying something like "It's not fair! You deserved that honor more than she did!"

My internal voices are sometimes much clearer. In a heated discussion with a parishioner who arrogantly insisted I should preach from the pulpit instead of roaming around the chancel, I seemed to hear a much clearer message: "Don't bother trying to convince him. What's he know anyway? He's a (something not clear). Give him (might have been 'what for' but it might have been something else)!"

Sometimes the voice screams. When I noticed that the check-out girl at the counter had a very noticeable top of a tattoo peeping out at her neckline, my internal voice clearly said, "Can you guess what the rest of that tattoo looks like?" Then it got louder, "And what other ones she has?" Finally it shouted unmistakably, "And where?"

Naturally I didn't listen to the voice, even though it was insistent. But you can certainly understand why I don't want you to tell my bishop.

For a long time I didn't even realize that I was hearing these voices. A discussion with atheists about the supernatural enlightened me.

"Satan and devils and demons, all that supernatural stuff is balderdash," one of the atheists had derided. "It's all balderdash." (Actually it was a different, stronger word that sounds slightly like balderdash but has only two syllables and probably wouldn't be appropriate in a family paper.)

"Like that story about Satan tempting Jesus in the wilderness," said another.

That story, Matthew 4:1-11 and Luke 4: 1-13, had always intrigued me because it has absolutely no visual description of the Tempter, no account of horns or pitchfork or bat-like wings or hooves or pointed tail, and yet when people talk about Satan that's usually the picture they have in mind. In Matthew and Luke it's just a voice. I imagined Jesus simply hearing a voice in his head.

That's when I realized I hear voices in my head too. All the time, when I came to think about it. I explained that to my atheist friends, using examples such as the ones I gave above.

"That's not Satan influencing you," they reassured me. "That's just something out of your subconscious. It's not the same as Jesus' temptation. That was really Satan. The Bible says it was."

It turned out those atheists knew a lot more about the Bible than I did. They told me that though the Bible didn't actually say so, a figure in red with horns and a pitchfork was talking to Jesus, and since I hadn't seen such a figure it couldn't have been Satan talking to me.

I suggested that maybe Jesus' hearing a tempting voice was the same kind of experience as mine. They ridiculed me, claiming that if the Bible said it was Satan's voice, there must have been a figure in red with a pitchfork.

They went on to explain that I hadn't actually heard a supernatural voice in my head but that repressed impulses and primal urges and manifestations of my id had risen up unbidden from my subconscious. That frightened me more than if it had been the voice of Satan, Lucifer, and Beelzebul themselves.

I tried to point out that we don't really know where those voices in our heads come from. Maybe they're the sinister influences of malevolent supernatural

Intelligences. Or maybe they are leftover stuff from below or outside our normal awareness that suddenly comes to our attention. I could understand the voices-in-our-heads phenomenon on the basis of either of those models. Either way I wanted to go on from the theoretical question of their source to the practical question of how to resist them or make them stop.

My atheist friends kept insisting they were from the "Subconscious" and it would be unhealthy to make them stop because they were only natural and there was nothing wrong with them.

They didn't know what my voices sometimes suggested! (Your voice can be heard at bohmhome@shentel.net)

- - - - -

Having enjoyed musing along with the altar ego, you would enjoy the sequel volume, *Altar Ego Musings Too*. Visit the website, www.AltarEgoPub.com for information about its availability as well as for ordering information and a sample of the mystery novel, *Testing the Spirits*, in which a Lutheran pastor in Pennsylvania's Pocono mountains joins forces with a New Age shop owner when the shop and church are both vandalized with graffiti and there is a murderous attack on the police chief's son in a locked room situation. www.AltarEgoPub.com has information also and a sample of *Testing the Spirits'* sequel, *Gazing into Heaven*, in which an amateur astronomer in the Poconos is found dead in a locked observatory after discussing suicide with the pastor. Twelve short stories involving the same people as the novels will be available from www.AltarEgoPub.com under the title *Down the Line*. Finally, use www.AltarEgoPub.com or rkb@altaregopub.com to recruit the altar ego himself to present a workshop, lead a Bible study, give a lecture, preach a sermon, or even serve as interim pastor at your church.

Wholeness and holiness!
R K B

Printed in the United States
217415BV00002B/3/A